# Victoria

# DECORATING WITH A PERSONAL TOUCH

# Victoria

# DECORATING WITH A PERSONAL TOUCH

ALISON WORMLEIGHTON

HEARST BOOKS

A Division of Sterling Publishing Co., Inc.

New York

For Paul

Library of Congress Cataloging-in-Publication Data
Available upon request.

10  9  8  7  6  5  4  3  2  1

First Paperback Edition 2006
Published by Hearst Books
A Division of Sterling Publishing Co., Inc.
387 Park Avenue South, New York, NY 10016

*Hearst Books is proud to continue the superb style, quality, and tradition of* Victoria *magazine with every book we publish. On our beautifully illustrated pages you will always find inspiration and ideas about the subjects you love.*

For information about custom editions, special sales, premium and corporate purchases, please contact Sterling Special Sales Department at 800-805-5489 or specialsales@sterlingpub.com.

Distributed in Canada by Sterling Publishing
c/o Canadian Manda Group, 165 Dufferin Street
Toronto, Ontario, Canada M6K 3H6

Distributed in Australia by Capricorn Link (Australia) Pty. Ltd.
P.O. Box 704, Windsor, NSW 2756 Australia

Manufactured in China

Designed by Janet James

Sterling ISBN-13: 978-1-58816-569-5
ISBN 10: 1-58816-569-8

# CONTENTS

*continued over*

Whether you are planning a full-scale remodeling job that involves bringing in the professionals, or you want to make just a few crucial changes that will transform the look of a particular room, it's important to know what you like and how to achieve it. Using scale, color, pattern, and texture to make the most of your living space and establish your own decorating signature is the essence of interior design—no matter how large or small the project.

# INTRODUCTION

# PERSONAL STYLE

**RIGHT:** The entry hall is the first room visitors see, so make sure it expresses your preferences in color, pattern, and art.

**BELOW:** When planning your decorating scheme, don't forget practical spaces, such as the laundry room.

Your home is simultaneously your private space and your public face, and the only way it will work well at both levels is if you allow it to be a genuine expression of yourself. Aim to make it somewhere that reflects your personality—who you are, where you've been, what you like. Perhaps one or more rooms require a fairly dramatic transformation, while others need only a few minor tweaks. However drastic the facelift you are after for your home, the key to making changes that will suit you over the long term is to develop your own sense of style. Personal style is at the heart of any successful decorating scheme. It gives a room its special ambience, making it feel warm and welcoming, full of character and interest. At the same time, it insures that your home works for you—that it is comfortable, functional, and somewhere that you, your family, and your friends all feel at ease.

Some people seem to know instinctively what they like and how to achieve it in their own homes to dazzling effect, but for most of us the process is more gradual, as we glean ideas from a variety of sources and slowly piece together an individual style. It's tempting to follow the dictates of fashion in an attempt to short-circuit this process, particularly as fashions in interiors are now so high-profile and fast-changing. By all means, use the latest ideas pictured in magazines as inspiration to adapt to your own requirements. But don't adopt

## POWER OF OBSERVATION

To find out what interior styles you like best, start by simply looking around you:

- **Study pictures in books, and cut out and file pictures from magazines of your favorite looks. Analyze what you like about them.**
- **Look at homes that are the same age and architectural style as yours, to see what styles work best.**
- **Observe the way you use your home: Is informality crucial to you? Do you like to feel cozy or unencumbered? Basic attitudes like these affect your preferences in interiors.**

**LEFT:** Chintz and floral patterns have a timeless charm that is the secret of their enduring popularity. However much fashions change, there will always be a place for classic patterns.

fashions wholesale—you're not trying to impress your friends or parade your skills so much as to share with them the things that have a personal significance for you. At any rate, guests always prefer a relaxed and comfortable home to a showcase, however up-to-the-minute or impressive it is. Let your own personality shine through.

Sometimes only the smallest change is needed to give a room a lift. Imagination and ingenuity will have more impact than a large budget—you don't have to throw everything out and start from scratch to get the look you want. The possessions you have already accumulated are part of your personal identity, so keeping the ones you like best will be essential to creating a personal style. Also, as you acquire new possessions and your lifestyle and tastes alter in the future, your decor will accommodate them because it too will evolve. Overall, your home will still feel cohesive—a sign of a successful interior scheme—because your own decorating signature will provide the unifying element.

Another characteristic of a successful scheme is that it manages to look uncontrived, and the way to achieve this is to believe in every effect you create. Gradually, as you become more familiar with interior design techniques, and become acquainted with the range of options open to you, you will gain confidence in your own decorating skills. Learning to trust your eye and your instincts is the secret of all successful design.

**ABOVE RIGHT:** Making a personal style statement becomes much easier if you have cleared away the unnecessary clutter.

**RIGHT:** Creating a personal style is not limited to permanent fixtures and fittings. Setting a table for a special meal allows you to express your creativity.

# ANALYZING YOUR HOME

The first step toward developing your home's potential is to look closely at what you will be working with. You need to assess what is there already, what works (or could be made to work), and what you don't like, as well as what you are likely to need in the future. You can then rearrange or refurbish and even reuse a lot of it, all the while planning each step carefully. You will keep better control over your budget and timetable than if you worked in a less restrained way. You will also probably wind up with a look that is closer to what you really like. In the end you may discover that the only new element that was needed was ingenuity.

If, on the other hand, you are starting from scratch, the process can seem quite daunting, since you have such a vast array of options. Even so, you probably have some cherished possessions that you want to incorporate, and one or two of these may provide a suitable starting point. Draw up a plan of action, breaking it down into logical, "bite-size" stages so that the entire project will be less daunting and more manageable.

However minor the refurbishment you are planning, consider whether any structural work should be part of it. There's little point in making only cosmetic changes if something is fundamentally wrong with the room that could easily be put

## USER FRIENDLY

When planning major refurbishment, always keep in mind how your home will be used. Ask yourself questions like the following:

- **Where do you like to relax and eat?**
- **How many people will use the home?**
- **Will the home be used by children or an elderly person?**
- **Do you have pets?**
- **What are the main traffic patterns through the home?**
- **How do you like to entertain, how often, and how many guests do you usually have at one time?**
- **If you have children, where will they play and entertain their friends?**

**FAR LEFT:** A sample board, also sometimes called a color board, is a visual aid used by interior designers. Collect samples of all the fabrics, trimmings, wallpapers, flooring, and paints, plus, where possible, photographs or drawings of furniture you plan to buy. Cut out pieces of the samples and stick them to a large piece of cardboard, writing the name, number, color, supplier, and price next to each sample.

**LEFT:** When planning furniture layouts, take into account (human) traffic patterns through each room. In an entry hall, a table surface and somewhere to sit down are invaluable, but make sure they are not in the way.

right. For instance, if the room is dark, think about enlarging it or adding a window or French doors leading to the backyard. Consider changing or adding architectural elements, moving radiators, or building in some extra storage.

Think about the room in the context of the rest of the house: Would an additional room, such as another bathroom, a utility room, a dressing room, a hobby room, or a den, dramatically improve your life? Perhaps you could make an existing, underused room do double duty, or partition off part of a large room to create a new space. Maybe removing a wall would turn two cramped rooms into a functional area. Even though these alterations will probably evolve over a long period of time, it's worth having an overview from the beginning, as what you do to a room now may affect your future plans for other parts of the home.

Once you know the framework on which your whole room design will hang, you need to plan the furniture arrangement (see page 61) before you go any further. The easiest way to do this is to measure the room and make a scale drawing of it. Measure the furniture (including any you have yet to buy) and make paper or cardboard templates for each piece. Now simply shuffle the pieces around your floor plan. Once you have worked this out, you can finalize your lighting plan and tackle the room's decor.

**RIGHT:** Architectural elements and built-in furniture or storage areas, like this wall-to-wall bookcase, are your starting points when planning any space.

**BELOW LEFT:** Think about a room's function before you plan any changes. If you want to work in it, for example, you'll need to include space for a table and chair near a good source of natural light, plus built-in lighting or outlets for lamps to light the table.

## MAKING PLANS

Follow this sequence when planning a room makeover:

- **First, think about the "bare bones" of the room and plan any structural changes.**
- **Next, plan the arrangement of the furniture, using a floor plan and templates.**
- **Consider the lighting and plan any changes, incorporating light fixtures, switches, and outlets in your floor plan.**
- **Finally, choose the interior decorating style, preparing a sample board if possible.**

# SPACE & LIGHT

It's important to make optimum use of space and light in any decor. Light defines a space, so the two are inextricably bound together. To see both of these aspects of a room clearly, imagine it empty, and examine the architecture that encloses the space, the view out of the window, and the light coming in. Consider what you can do to maximize this light (for example, using light colors and mirrors, avoiding too heavy curtains) while at the same time controlling it: Sunlight usually needs to be filtered (see pages 46–7), and softened by reflecting it off surfaces. Decide what the room's strongest and weakest points are so that you'll know what you want to play up or down.

Physically, of course, space is crucial to a room, in terms not only of size but also of shape, since these can affect how functional it is. Sometimes problems are resolved easily, for example by hinging a door on the other side so that you don't have to walk around it; or changing a closet door to a sliding door to prevent it from being in the way when it's open. In other cases, however, the only solutions are aesthetic—to make a space look bigger, smaller, or better-proportioned than it really is, use sleight of hand.

For example, a room that was formerly two rooms may look too long and narrow, but various visual tricks can dramatically offset this. Paint or wallpaper the end walls in a warm, "advancing" color and the sides in a cool, "receding" color (see page 28). Break up the length with an archway, place pictures and mirrors on the long walls, and position chairs and tables (but not long pieces of furniture like sofas) against them. Lines that stretch away from the eye make a room look longer, while lines set across the line of vision have

**LEFT:** The fact that this entry hall is small is scarcely noticeable because of the pared-down furnishings and the view of the light-filled room through the doorway.

**BELOW:** In a big room, furnishings need to be large in scale so as not to be dwarfed by the room.

## SMALL AND BEAUTIFUL

Small spaces can be made to seem bigger using a variety of ploys

- **Reduce unnecessary furniture and clutter.**
- **Include the occasional oversize piece of furniture (see pages 22–3).**
- **Match the furniture to the walls.**
- **Use a light, cool color on the walls and ceiling, and wash the walls with light (see pages 80–3).**
- **Incorporate some reflective surfaces such as mirrored walls.**
- **Consider a trompe l'oeil mural.**
- **Maximize the amount of light.**
- **Illuminate an area in the distance—it makes the space in front of it seem larger.**
- **Fit flooring with a diagonal pattern.**

the opposite effect, so avoid the lengthwise lines (chair rails or strip flooring running the length of the room) and exploit the crosswise ones (long seating placed against the end walls).

You can also use sleight of hand to make ceilings appear higher, for example by painting the ceiling in a tone slightly lighter than the walls (possibly with a shimmer paint) and by using full-length curtains and vertical stripes on the walls. To make a too-high ceiling seem lower, paint it in a shade slightly darker than the walls; fit a chair rail and paint the walls beneath it a darker color than the walls above. Similar tricks are possible to make rooms look bigger or smaller (see boxes on pages 19 and this page, right).

How a space is used is actually more important than its size. In fact, having some unused space in a room gives you a sense of freedom. For the same reason, consider any adjoining rooms when planning a redecoration project, since a home works best when the spaces seem to flow into each other. Think how one room will look from another, and plan your decorating accordingly.

## IN LARGE MEASURE

Use these techniques to bring cavernous spaces down in scale:

- **Subdivide the area, using flooring, furniture groupings, lighting, color, shelving, columns, large plants, screens, panels of fabric, or sliding screens of translucent glass.**
- **Introduce a repeated element that sets up a visual rhythm, breaking up the space while creating a more ordered feeling.**

**LEFT:** Light is one of the most precious elements in a room, so choose window treatments that make the most of it, ranging from louvers, shutters, or sheer curtains or shades that filter the light, to absolutely nothing at all, as in this room.

**FAR LEFT:** Subdividing a room into separate zones using furniture groupings or lighting makes it cozier.

# SCALE & BALANCE

In interior design, scale refers to the size of something relative to the size of a room, the architectural features, and the other furnishings, and also its overall balance in a room. The need for balance is part of human nature, and creating a visual balance in each room makes for a more harmonious home. If you like the individual elements in a room but they just don't seem to look right together, it's probably the scale of the furnishings that has gone wrong. Sometimes simply rearranging furniture or perhaps adding or removing a piece is enough to create a balanced look, while at other times more drastic action may be needed.

Aim for the height and visual weight of a room's furnishings to be varied and also to be in equilibrium, creating an overall harmony. If there are too many heavy-looking elements, the room will look ponderous, but if there are not enough of them it may look insubstantial. Similarly, too many tall elements will make a room seem stiff and

**LEFT:** Arrange small framed pictures together rather than hanging them individually so that the scale of the group they form is balanced with the chair or other piece of furniture they may be above. Balance is also important when you hang a large picture or mirror, as it should not be larger than the piece of furniture it is adjacent to.

## IN THE BALANCE

Scale is an attribute of a room's furniture, architectural features, floors, window treatments, walls—in other words, everything. Here are some examples:

- *Tall*: armoire, wall unit, tall plant, high-backed seating, large painting or mirror
- *Low*: low bookshelf, chest of drawers, small plant, low-backed seating, landscape-shape painting or mirror hung low
- *Heavy*: armoire, piano, upholstery, elaborate window treatments, Oriental rug, dark walls or furniture
- *Light*: occasional chairs, cane seating, étagère, sheer curtains, needlepoint or plain rug, pale walls or furniture

formal, while having too few will make it look incomplete and squat. You don't have to contrive a precise 50/50 split for each attribute—just be aware of the need to balance the scale of furnishings while at the same time varying them.

Interior designers always recommend that you scale up rather than down—in other words, don't be afraid of overscaling (also known as oversizing). In a small room, small-scale pieces simply look bland. Including some large-scale pieces is preferable, because it makes the room seem more important, tricking the eye into thinking there must be more space than there really is. You can then also include some small items (but not a lot), by massing them so that they borrow the scale of the group of which they are a part. In a large room, you should also overscale, but even more so because everything about the room is bigger.

By being brave and having a few large "anchor pieces" or features that take the eye upward, such as full-height doors (or doors with pictures above them), you will create a more memorable room. Be bold and generous throughout, in everything from the mirror over the fireplace to the fringe on a cushion. Some designers would say that taking risks with scale is the secret of successful design.

**ABOVE:** A large and dramatic, beautifully proportioned staircase makes a sweeping statement in this entry hall.

# COLOR SCHEMES

Color is the quickest and most dramatic way to transform a room, whether it involves a whole new color scheme or just a few carefully chosen accents. Because colors speak directly to the emotions, they are the aspect of interior decorating that elicits the most personal response. Once you are conversant with the properties of colors and have discovered what color combinations you like, you can start introducing them to your home. In many cases this will not involve re-covering all the furniture or redecorating throughout, but simply painting one wall or adding a few carefully chosen items that will give the whole room a lift.

All color starts with three primary colors that cannot be mixed from other colors; in pigments and dyes these are red, yellow, and blue. When pairs of primaries are mixed together in equal proportions, they form the three secondary colors, orange, green, and violet. Arranging these six colors around a circle in the sequence in which they appear in a rainbow (with each secondary color between the two primary colors from which it was formed) produces a simple color wheel. Mixing equal proportions of adjacent pairs of colors (ie, a primary mixed with a secondary color) produces six tertiary colors, which can be shown on a color wheel containing 12 segments (see below).

These colors, or hues, are all of maximum intensity and purity. When lightened with white, they are called tints, and when darkened with black they become shades. When they have gray (ie, both black and white) added, they are midtones. Tints, midtones, and shades are collectively known as tones (although, confusingly, "tone" is often used

## COLOR PLAY

If you are nervous about using a strong color on your walls, try one of these ploys:

- **For a modern look, paint just one wall in the stronger color.**
- **Use the color behind a bookcase to lessen the impact.**
- **Choose a wall with plenty of doors, windows, moldings, or staircases, as these will break up the expanse of color.**
- **Use your chosen color in a transitional space of the home, such as a hallway or stairwell.**

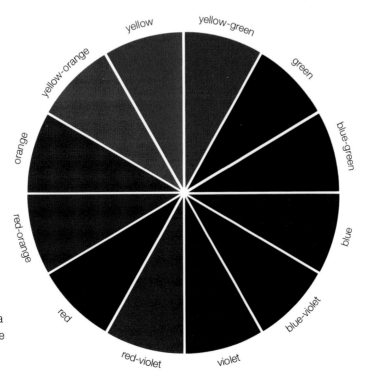

**LEFT:** Colors are affected by incoming light as well as artificial light. The light itself changes throughout the day and with the seasons. The direction the windows face also affects it and so color schemes may need to be warmer or cooler to compensate. Latitude is yet another factor, which is why bold hues that can look wonderful in southern California or Florida don't always translate to New England.

**LEFT:** The color wheel illustrates how colors are interrelated. Each triangular segment shows a primary, secondary, or tertiary color. These are the unadulterated hues, without any black, gray, or white added. Pairs of colors exactly opposite each other on the wheel are known as complementary colors.

**LEFT:** Color ideas can come from anywhere, but nature offers one of the best sources of inspiration. Here the green foliage combined with reddish-pink flowers in a blue cup is echoed by the green curtain against the blue wall with reddish-pink in the tablecloth pattern.

**RIGHT:** This gentle palette of softened contrasts— in this case, tints of the complementary colors red and green—combined with white is a far cry from the dramatic contrast of the undiluted hues.

simply as a synonym for midtone or even for color). The neutrals black, gray, and white do not appear on a color wheel because they are not colors.

Colors on the red side of the wheel are "warm," while those on the blue side are "cool." Warm colors look as though they are advancing toward you slightly, while cool colors appear to be receding. As a result, warm schemes are cozy and intimate, while cool schemes are restful and refreshing.

For many people, devising color schemes is the essence of interior decorating, and the color wheel provides a good way to understand the different types of palettes that can be used. "Adjacent" (or "related" or "harmonious") color schemes are made up of between three and five colors adjacent to each other (and possibly also the odd contrasting accent). You could use a favorite color plus one or two colors on each side of it on the wheel. "Monochromatic" palettes are based on several tones of just one color, though in practice these are usually combined with a neutral and a few small touches of accent colors. Similar to these are schemes using neutral colors. All of these schemes are very restful and relaxing and so are ideal for living rooms and bedrooms.

"Contrasting" schemes involve hues that are on opposite sides of the wheel. These can be just roughly opposite each other, or in precise positions, as with the "complementary" scheme, which is made up of a pair of complementary hues. Exactly opposite each other on the color wheel, complementary pairs have the maximum amount of contrast and so are dynamic and high-energy. However, for this type of palette to look right in a room, the two complementary colors should not be used in equal amounts, or they will fight for attention. Allowing one color—normally the cooler one—to predominate defuses the tension between them. Also, they need to be used with white or another neutral to create "breathing space."

Another type of contrasting palette, known as a split-complementary scheme, combines a hue with the colors adjacent to its complement, such as red with yellow-green and blue-green. The contrasting scheme known as a triadic scheme combines three hues that are equidistant on the wheel—such as the three primaries (red, yellow, blue), the three secondaries (green, orange, violet), or three equidistant tertiaries (yellow-green, blue-violet, red-orange; or blue-green, red-violet, yellow-orange). These boldly contrasting palettes are not usually relaxing enough for living rooms and bedrooms, but they can work well where you want a stimulating atmosphere such as an entry hall, home office, or child's room.

More versatile are color schemes made up of "softened contrasts," in which some or all of the contrasting hues are replaced with tones (ie, tints, midtones, or shades) of those hues. Palettes including contrasting tints are fresh and cheerful, but it's the combinations of contrasting midtones and shades that are the most complex and subtle. Colors that have been subdued, through the addition of black or a dark earth color to the basic hues, are sometimes called "knocked back" or "dirtied" colors.

**LEFT:** Light, serene, and restful, the blue-and-white color scheme used in this spacious room extends to everything, including the white-painted floorboards. The only slight deviation is the sand color of the woven chair back, which emphasizes the texture and enriches the scheme considerably.

**BELOW:** By covering up the dark wood of the tabletop, a simple white cloth transforms this still life. Without it, the tones would have been in the gloomy range.

**LEFT:** The only dark tone in this room, the small table nevertheless serves to anchor the neutral palette and keep the look grounded.

**RIGHT:** This room is lively and full of verve, with both color contrast in the red and white, and tonal contrast between the white and the fairly deep tones of the red.

It's important for any color scheme to have tonal balance, between the light, mid, and dark tones. Tonal contrasts are important because they create the underlying visual framework, yet this is an area in which color schemes often fall down. Sometimes adjusting the tonal balance wakes up the entire decor. Tone is dependent upon the amount of white, gray, or black that has been added to the pure hues, but some colors, such as yellow, look light even without the addition of white, while others, such as violet, look dark without any black being added. In a black and white photograph of a room (or a photocopy of any of the pictures in this book) the tones become apparent, so try to imagine what colors would look like if reproduced in black and white. Any color scheme that has only light tones could look anemic, one with only midtones bland, and one with dark tones gloomy. However, in a room with a lot of color

## PROS' PRACTICES

Take a leaf from the professionals when using color in your home:

- **Use several tones of the same color to enhance carving or moldings on coves or around doorways.**
- **Paint woodwork with a softer tone of the wall color, the same color in a satin finish, or a muted ivory tone. A darker shade can be used for the baseboard if you prefer, to define the shape of the room.**
- **Pick up a color in a painting and repeat it on a larger scale elsewhere.**
- **Don't be over-zealous in color matching. Interior designers build in the occasional mismatch to add piquancy and prevent a room from looking too static or "designed."**

contrasts, the tonal contrasts will need to be played down, to compensate. Likewise, in a scheme with few color contrasts, tonal contrasts will be more important.

One decorating approach is to use a deep tone for the floor, a midtone for the walls, a slightly lighter midtone for the ceiling, and the lightest tone for the woodwork. By choosing relatively plain colors that will be easy to live with as the base colors for walls and window treatments and then layering more exciting colors on top (in upholstery or slipcover fabrics, pillows, trimmings, rugs, lampshades, picture mats, and other accessories), your decor will be much more flexible and long-lived. Accents can be used to add sharp zingy color. Flashes of vibrant color pack more of a visual punch when used in small doses against a sophisticated, muted background of neutrals than an excess of loud colors ever could.

If your home is large, having distinct color palettes for each room is feasible, provided the floor coverings and wall colors don't clash where they meet and the views from open doors into adjoining rooms are also harmonious. In a small home, however, it is often better to use an overall palette of colors, varying the proportions from room to room.

If a particular room is dark and dingy, many designers believe that there is little point in struggling to make it a little lighter. Instead, accept the room's limitations, making a feature of them by creating a cozy atmosphere with rich, jewel colors. The overall feeling can always be brightened by light-colored accents and lightened by white woodwork if necessary. By the same token, a light, airy room will benefit from the use of light, airy colors—as will a small room, which will be made to feel more spacious.

**RIGHT:** An example of an adjacent color scheme, this room predominantly features tones of blue and lilac, with green accents. White prevents the look from becoming overbearing.

# PATTERN & TEXTURE

The skillful use of pattern and texture brings a room to life. Pattern adds richness and vigor and provides a basis around which the entire space can be designed. Modernists have tended to eschew pattern in favor of broad expanses of flat color, and as a result its use today is less lavish than in previous decades, but there is a place for pattern in any interior. A fabric, wallpaper, rug, or carpet containing several colors offers a great way to unify a decor, as you can pick out the colors in the pattern to use throughout the room or in adjoining rooms. If you have various items you'd like to include, seek out a fabric that incorporates the colors of these items to unify them instantly. Likewise, if you have a favorite object or piece of art that you'd like to design the room around, find a pattern that contains the same colors and use it as the starting point for the decor.

If you are unsure about introducing pattern into a room, the safest approach is to use just one (whether in fabric, wallpaper, rug, or carpet), balancing it with toning solid colors. This is the way pattern is often used by interior designers today—boldly and sparingly, avoiding busy, dispersed pattern and instead featuring just one or two big design statements.

**RIGHT:** Patterns in different scales can be layered to add richness and depth to a decorating scheme.

**BELOW:** A mixture of floral patterns in different scales and colors is sharpened by a bold stripe upholstery on a chair.

Mixing patterns can produce a warm, cozy look. If you want to avoid too riotous an effect, however, create a visual break with a solid color between two patterns (choosing a color that appears in both, or using white). Even just a chair rail between two patterned wallpapers, or a baseboard between a patterned carpet and wallpaper, can be enough. To combine patterns successfully, remember that there should be both a link in color and a contrast in scale. Large, dominant patterns will fight for attention, so you will want only one of these in a room (or at most two, provided they are similar in color and mood). You can, however, have several smaller prints, so long as they are different in scale. Patterns that are very similar can sometimes be successfully combined (particularly if they are the same pattern in reversed colors, such as red-on-white and white-on-red), but normally the actual patterns as well as their scale should contrast.

It is possible to purchase a fabric and a wallpaper in the same pattern and colors, but the two materials rarely

match exactly, and this approach is considered dated. Similarly, coordinated patterns that have been designed for use together tend to seem just too planned and perfect. To look right, the effect should be more haphazard, as if serendipity had produced such an interesting combination. Along with modern fabrics you could even include an old fabric from a needlework cushion, vintage quilt, or antique textile, to create a more eclectic mix.

The easiest way to plan the decor is to start with the dominant pattern; next, find two or three small- and

**LEFT:** Red and white toile de Jouy is unsurpassed in creating a romantic atmosphere for a bedroom.

medium-scale patterns to use with it (unless you are using just one pattern in the room); and then decide which solid colors you want to use with them. Large patterns usually look best on the biggest surfaces in a room—the walls, floors, and window treatments. Bear in mind that a two-color pattern without much contrast between the background and the motif will be more subtle than a multicolored design with a lot of contrast. Medium-size patterns can be used for upholstery or slipcovers. Small patterns look wishy-washy spread over a large area and if viewed from across the room simply seem to disappear, so restrict their use to items such as pillows and chair seats (or walls/floor in a very small room). When you are making your selections, keep in mind that any of the fabrics and wall and floor coverings may look bland on their own, but when combined they will create a balanced decor; if each of these elements has too much punch the overall effect could be overpowering.

A variety of textures is, of course, found in all rooms, but textural contrast can be a creative and useful tool in interior design, particularly in rooms decorated in neutral solid colors or understated patterns. Although too many textural contrasts can be distracting, an interesting mix of textures will undoubtedly enhance a decor. The texture of the floor often dominates a room, so be aware of this when considering studded rubber, rough limestone, a soft pile carpet, or any other option. You can add texture to walls (see opposite), but the furniture, fabrics, and accessories are where you can indulge yourself, even if it's as simple as a silk-bordered linen curtain hanging from a wrought-iron pole.

**BELOW:** The textures of polished wood and sheer fabric are enhanced by the absence of color and pattern in this entry hall. Textural contrasts are particularly effective in neutral schemes like this.

## TYPES OF PATTERNS

Patterns are usually grouped into several types:

- **Geometrics—checks and stripes—are terrific mixers with any pattern, including themselves, and are the easiest to decorate with.**
- **Florals are always popular and are easy to use. Retro-style 1950's designs and faded shabby-chic effects have been particularly fashionable in recent years. To prevent them from looking too sugary, mix them with geometrics.**
- **Pictorials, such as toile de Jouy, are so distinctive and elaborate that they can be difficult to combine with other patterns. They don't go well with florals but look great with geometrics.**
- **Eclectics—such as animal prints, plaid tartans, chinoiserie (Chinese-inspired) styles, and ethnic patterns—are so dramatic and exotic that they make excellent focal points in a room. Surprising combinations can inject humor. However, eclectics do not create a subtle effect.**

### THE ROUGH WITH THE SMOOTH

With a delectable range of textures, baskets offer an effortless way to enrich your interiors, as well as supremely flexible storage space. Rough textures, like this storage box, lend a rustic and countrified look, particularly in combination with cane and bamboo, as on this chest of drawers.

### WALLPAPER PLUS

Add texture to walls with wall coverings such as paper-backed burlap (shown here), grass-cloth, foil, woven raffia, felt, woven hemp, silk, cork, wood veneer, or real or imitation suede or leather. Bear in mind, however, that such wall coverings tend to be delicate and difficult to clean.

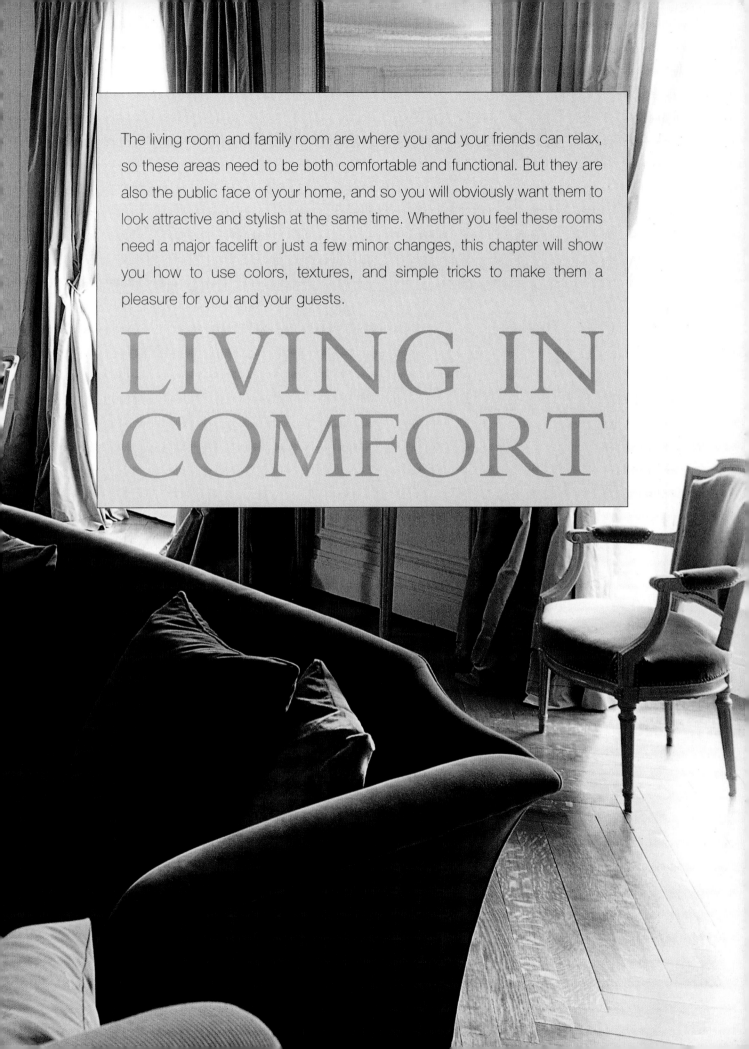

The living room and family room are where you and your friends can relax, so these areas need to be both comfortable and functional. But they are also the public face of your home, and so you will obviously want them to look attractive and stylish at the same time. Whether you feel these rooms need a major facelift or just a few minor changes, this chapter will show you how to use colors, textures, and simple tricks to make them a pleasure for you and your guests.

# LIVING IN COMFORT

# NEUTRAL COLOR SCHEMES

**LEFT:** In a white scheme, slipcovers are a more practical choice than upholstery. The informality of these cotton slipcovers counteracts any austerity. They are a simple way to introduce a white scheme to existing furniture, and create a background for scatter pillows in accent colors.

The best living rooms are comfortable and informal yet stylish, with color schemes that support these roles. A neutral scheme is most suitable for a room like this, where you spend a lot of time. Depending on your present decor, it may be possible for you to achieve it with just a lick of paint and a set of slipcovers. If your floor and window treatments are not neutral, you could still create a scheme based around neutrals but incorporating your existing colors: The beauty of neutral tones is that they look good with virtually any color.

Neutral schemes are based on shades of black, brown, gray, taupe, beige, cream, or white, enlivened with splashes of bright accent colors. The palette may be either warm or cool, according to the neutral shades you choose. Neutrals do not attract attention, so texture and tonal contrast become more important than usual.

The ultimate neutral, white, is a perennial favorite—not surprisingly, as it goes with everything, looks fresh and chic, and never goes out of fashion. However, a balance of light, medium, and dark tones is important in any scheme, and white is no exception. The rich browns of wood floors, furniture, and unpainted woodwork, while still maintaining the neutral scheme, provide a good contrast with the white and prevent the effect from being too bland.

## MATERIAL BENEFITS

Most neutrals echo the tones of organic materials, which is why wood, stone, wicker and rattan, leather, and fabrics like linen and wool complement neutral palettes so well. One of the joys of neutral colors is that the wonderful textures of these materials are enhanced.

A predominantly white room can be trickier to handle than you would think, so follow these tips:

- **Splashes of colors enliven white, but as white makes colors seem to jump out, use these accents sparingly.**
- **Use two, three, or even four shades of off-white to prevent a harsh or monotonous effect.**
- **To give the room a lift, use the lightest tone on the cove or ceiling and the darkest on the baseboard.**

**IN TOUCH**
Including a variety of textures is essential in neutral schemes, and it's very easy to do. Nubby wool blankets and pillows, cozy fleece throws, and richly polished wood floors provide a delightfully tactile array of textures here.

**LEFT:** Classic stripes emphasize the symmetry of this well-proportioned room, for a look that is dramatic, yet still restrained.

Neutral schemes are known for being calm, understated, and undemanding, but, in fact, the more contrast they incorporate, the more dramatic the effect. While white-on-white is soft and romantic, a crisp black-and-white scheme is upbeat and dynamic. Indeed, black and white provide the ultimate contrast.

Stripes, like checks, look good with other geometric patterns—try mixing stripes with stripes in a different scale but the same colors, or with checks or even polkadots. The neutral colors will prevent them from looking childish. Stripes also work well with florals and with finely etched pictorial patterns such as toile de Jouy in the same color combination. As with clothing, stripes are useful for creating illusions. Used vertically, they will make a room seem taller, while wide horizontal stripes will make a long, narrow room look less like a corridor. Bold stripes add a sense of order or formality to a room—but, perhaps even more important, they add panache.

**BOTTOM RIGHT:** Bold stripes make this chair an elegant focal point, but the restrained color choice allows the fabric to work with the neutral look.

Black and white look striking on their own, but they also go beautifully with rich golden brown. Reminiscent of nineteenth-century Biedermeier furniture, crafted in ebony and maple or cherry wood, this color combination gives a living room a look of sophistication. These neutrals are wonderful by themselves, but neutrals can also be used in a supporting role for other colors, for example juxtaposed with a vibrant feature wall. Also, small amounts of black will sharpen up any color scheme.

**MAINTAINING NEUTRALITY**
Plants fit into any color scheme, as the green of their foliage is rarely intrusive. Architectural plants like this bamboo are particularly effective, as the outline and texture of the foliage contrast with the straight lines of the furniture.

# WALLS

Even if you do not want a completely neutral color palette, it is sensible to use neutral, or at least muted, tones on the walls, floors, and windows of a room you use a lot, like the living room or family room, because they are low-key, undemanding, versatile colors that you are unlikely to tire of. You can then use stronger colors in the elements that are relatively easy to change, like flowers, pillows, lamps, pictures, and upholstery. If, however, you like to be surrounded by color, then follow your instincts and allow it onto your walls.

In the living room, which is not subjected to such hard wear as the family room, kitchen, or bathroom, you can indulge yourself with a wall covering that is less robust than elsewhere. Depending on your tastes, you could add luscious textures to the neutral tones with real or imitation suede or leather, or with paper-backed grass-cloth, foil, felt, silk, cork, wood veneer, or burlap. Lavish effects are also possible using fabric on the walls (see page 153).

For a simpler effect, walls can be paneled from floor to ceiling and then painted, stained, or left natural. A variation of this is to mount a chair rail or picture rail on the walls, and add a wainscot beneath this; on the wall above it, use fabric, paint, or wallpaper. Or omit the wainscot, and beneath the rail simply paint the wall in a contrasting color.

Walls given a velvety matte finish with latex (emulsion) or latex velvet (vinyl silk), set off by white woodwork, provide a perfect background for pictures and textiles. Or, for a dramatic look, try a specialist paint—from chalky calcimine (distemper) or creamy casein or milk paint to metallic, pearlized, or sparkle paints. Another possibility is one of the faux paint finishes, ranging from subtle effects such as faux stone, marble, leather, and wood to elaborate trompe l'oeil architectural features, moldings, and murals. Or you may like the soft shine of polished plaster containing marble dust.

Wallpaper, too, is available in faux effects—anything from imitation paint finishes to trompe l'oeil bookshelves—as well as a vast range of patterns. Small patterns lose their definition when seen at a distance, so they work best in small rooms. In living rooms and family rooms, where you spend a lot of time, it is safer to avoid very strong patterns, as they can be overpowering and you are likely to tire of them quickly. Nevertheless, if you fall in love with an amazing, strongly patterned wallpaper, you will probably be happy to allow it to dominate, and it might produce exactly the effect you want.

**ABOVE:** Elegant stripes in the hallway add pattern while keeping the overall color scheme neutral. Using the same color in the living room adds continuity throughout the public areas of the home, but the painted faux-stone effect on the walls adds a pleasing textural contrast.

**LEFT:** A chair rail provides an ideal opportunity to introduce an accent color. Here, a darker blue color on the wall beneath the chair rail and on the door helps to make a tall room feel more intimate, while still looking bright and light.

# WINDOW TREATMENTS

The right window treatment can instantly bring an interior up to date. These days, a grandiose, swagged treatment really only looks right when the room is equally grand —today's styles are generally much simpler (and easier to achieve).

If privacy, control over incoming light, and heat insulation aren't important, you might want to dispense with curtains or shades entirely. Leaving windows bare usually works best if they are attractive architecturally and if they frame a good view. At night, though, a bare window looms up dark and forbidding, unless you have outside lighting, so you might want to move a freestanding screen in front of it, which would also provide some privacy. A valance or simple scarf drapery across the top of a bare window is a good way of softening the effect.

Many leading designers are using window treatments consisting of two or three layers of translucent fabric, to filter the sunlight and provide privacy while letting in plenty of daylight and creating gorgeous contrasts of color or texture. The layers

## QUICK TRICKS

Give old curtains or shades a new lease on life with one of these ideas:

- **Stitch a contrasting border to the leading (inner) and lower curtain edges.**
- **Add some snazzy trimmings, such as crystal beads or tassels, colored feathers, large sequins, a deep bullion fringe, braid, or ribbons in different colors and widths.**
- **Appliqué a contrasting panel or full-length band down the center of a curtain or shade.**

**LEFT:** Generous light-colored sheer curtains let in the light, but still look opulent in this traditional-style room.

might consist of anything from different-colored panels of muslin slung over curtain poles, to silk or semi-sheer linen curtains combined with linen shades or venetian blinds.

Traditional curtain fabrics like cotton damask, linen, chenille, or silk taffeta always look superb in living rooms, but materials that are not normally associated with windows can also look fantastic. Try wool suiting, sari fabric, or the new synthetics, which range from imitation suedes and leathers to metallic meshes and sheers woven with fiberglass.

Before deciding on a window treatment, consider your requirements.

● Do you need to filter out strong sunlight in order to protect upholstery? If so, you could use either sheer curtains, lace panels, café curtains, translucent shades, or

Japanese-style paper screens. Blinds or shutters would also be effective in this situation.

● How much privacy do you want? A single layer of sheer fabric will provide privacy by day, but possibly not when the lights are on, so will you need more than one layer, or perhaps a thicker fabric?

● Curtains that are not full-length don't usually look right (unless they are within the window recess), so if there is a radiator under the window, then a shade, blind, or shutters might be preferable.

Think, too, about what style of window treatment would best suit your decor.

● Is there enough room on both sides of the window for curtains to be pulled back? If not, a single curtain, tied back in one asymmetric curve, might work better than a pair of curtains. Or, once again, a shade, a blind, or shutters might be preferable.

● Blinds, roller and roman shades, and shutters give a crisp, tailored look, while curtains create a softer look. Those that are, in effect, two straight columns of fabric will add a pleasing vertical element, but do you prefer the bold curves of curtains that meet in the center and are tied back?

● Do you want a color that will stand out or one that will blend in with the rest of the decor, making the room look more spacious?

● Consider trimmings for your window treatments at the same time as you choose your fabric. There are a wide variety of trimmings available, and you may even find one you like so much that you want to use it as your starting point for the window treatment—or even for the room's entire decor.

Before selecting the fabric, you'll need to decide upon the style details.

● What style of heading do you prefer? Self-styling tapes, which are stitched to the tops of curtains, have woven-in cords that are pulled up to create pleats or other decorative effects. On formal curtains, however,

**VINTAGE CHARM**
Vintage textiles ranging from small embroidered guest towels to linen sheets make charming curtains. Simplicity is the keynote, so hang the fabric from a pole using clip-on rings (see below), and make a feature of any decorative edging. An old-fashioned clothespin to hold it back is a nice touch.

You could use a contrasting fabric such as a stripe or check, then tie the curtains back to show it off. Lining is not suitable, however, for a floaty, translucent effect.

Don't forget "accessories" such as rods or poles and tiebacks. Curved rods hold the curtains away from the window, making them look important. Separate rods or poles for layered curtains allow them to be opened and closed individually. Because cornices (pelmets) that cover rods are no longer widely used, poles are increasingly popular, whether in wood, wrought iron, metal, or plexiglas. The finials are often extremely decorative in their own right. Tiebacks are innovative, too, ranging from silk ropes with large, theatrical tassels to braided string ropes or sparkly metal chains.

hand-made pinch pleats look better. There are many informal ways to hang curtains from poles, including clip-on rings (which are suitable only for lightweight fabric), jumbo grommets, ties, and tabs (see page 162). Many of the fancier headings are stationary, which means that the curtains will have to be decorative.

● How full do you want the curtains to be? For most styles, apart from panels, a fullness of two to three times the width of the pole or rod is recommended.

● Do you want the curtains to puddle generously onto the floor, or to just skim the floor? Both lengths are fashionable, but the former will get dirty much faster, particularly if you have children or pets.

● Lining will help protect them from the sun and provide good insulation. It is ideal for country-house-style curtains, particular if you interline them as well.

**RIGHT:** Sheer lace curtains look pretty if softly gathered, like these curtains, or as flat panels. Though lightweight, these full-length curtains still give a luxurious feel to the room.

**BELOW:** Sash café curtains, stretched between thin rods at the top and bottom of each curtain, are neat and functional, giving privacy while allowing light through.

# THE RIGHT RUG

Your choice of rug will, of course, depend on your decor:

- **Oriental and needlepoint rugs are the perfect partners for fine antiques.**
- **Braided or hooked rugs and flat-woven kilims suit country furniture.**
- **Shaggy pile rugs such as Scandinavian ryas or Greek flokatis, as well as flat-woven Indian dhurries and rugs in modern geometric designs, look good in contemporary interiors.**

**ABOVE:** Natural-fiber matting can be used either as a rug with bound edges, as in this room, or wall to wall, and it suits most decorating styles. Available in various fibers, including coir, rush, sisal, seagrass, and jute, it comes in different woven patterns, such as herringbone and bouclé, and in a variety of colors.

**LEFT:** Slightly faded and worn Oriental rugs add color and coziness to traditionally decorated rooms and look wonderful on wooden floors.

**RIGHT:** The floor can be the main source of color and pattern. Plain white walls allow this wooden floor, with its boards stained alternately light and dark, to take center stage in the room.

# FLOORS

The floor in a living room or family room needs to be both durable and comfortable. If your existing floor is good-looking in its own right, then one or more rugs will add coziness while still showing off the floor itself. If the floor is concrete, you could cover it with medium- to heavy-duty wall-to-wall carpet (see page 188) or natural-fiber matting; or you could install a hard flooring on top, and use rugs over that. If your existing floor is softwood boards, it could be treated in any of these ways, depending on its condition, or sanded down and then stained or painted.

Rugs are really useful in linking individual pieces of furniture, whether it is one rug in a small room, or more than one defining the seating areas and activity zones of a larger room. If there is already a lot of pattern in the room, a plain or subtly patterned rug will look better than one with a strong pattern. By the same token, a patterned rug in vibrant, strongly contrasting colors will make itself the focal point of a room. Any patterned rug should ideally incorporate some of the colors used elsewhere in the room. If you are designing a room from scratch, bear in mind that it's easier to start with the patterned rug and build the rest of the scheme around it.

## WOOD FLOORS

A wood floor looks good in any style of home and comes in various forms:

- **Wood block, parquet, or strip flooring is stylish enough for the living room and low-maintenance enough for the family room.**
- **Veneers are cheaper than solid wood, but also less hard-wearing, so choose a thick veneer.**
- **Architectural salvage stores sell reclaimed wood flooring which looks nicely aged.**

# FIREPLACES & MANTELS

"Hearth" and "Home" are inseparable concepts, and the fireplace is at the heart of the living room and family room. It is the natural focus, both visually and practically—indeed, the Latin word "*focus*" means "hearth" or "fireplace." Seating is arranged around the fireplace, collectibles accumulate on the mantelshelf, and the eye is inexorably drawn to the fire in the grate.

Mantelpieces, also known as fireplace surrounds, are traditionally made from marble, slate, or another stone, or from wood or cast iron. Each consists of a pair of jambs flanking the opening and supporting a frieze or lintel, on which the mantelshelf rests. If your fireplace is not as handsome as it ought to be, or has been removed entirely and the opening filled in, you may be able to replace it, as original and reproduction mantelpieces and grates are available. Bear in mind that measurements will be crucial, and the job has to be done prior to decorating.

You can choose from a variety of elegant styles, ranging from Federal-style wood mantelpieces to sleek contemporary stainless steel designs. However, because the fireplace is such a strong architectural feature in a room, choosing one that has the right proportions and is appropriate to your decor is important. If you live in a period home, architectural authenticity becomes a factor, too.

## COVER-UP JOB

When the fireplace is not in use, you may wish to cover or fill the opening in one of these ways:

- **Place a small folding screen, painted panel, cast-iron fireback, or metal grille in front of it.**
- **Arrange some chunky logs on the grate, or stand up some longer ones in front of the grate, filling most of the opening.**
- **On the hearth, place one or more large stone garden urns filled with logs, kindling, or pine cones. These could simply be moved when you light a fire.**

**RIGHT:** A roaring fire is the traditional focal point of a room, and nothing says "welcome home" in quite the same way.

**FAR RIGHT:** In the summer months, or when the fire is not in use, fill the opening with a flowering plant, greenery, dried flowers, large candles, or even a sculpture.

**RIGHT:** The paneled walls merge with the mantel of this splendid fireplace. In older houses, where the fire was originally the main source of light and heat, vast fireplaces often dominated the room.

If you are unable to replace the fireplace surround, there are other options open to you. You could apply fiberglass motifs or strips of beading or molding to the mantelpiece, or embellish a wooden mantel with painted decoration such as geometric patterns. Or you could make it less noticeable by painting it to match the other woodwork in the room.

If you don't have a fireplace at all, you could install a flueless fireplace, in the form of either a gel-flame fire, a flueless gas fire, or an electronic fireplace. Alternatively, you could simply create the effect of a fireplace, without the flames, by affixing a vintage mantelpiece to the wall, and then either filling the area between the jambs with a witty trompe l'oeil or big basket of dried flowers, or painting this area black and placing a pair of occasional chairs in front. Treat the mantelshelf and the wall above the dummy fireplace in the same way as for a real one. An even easier version of this is simply to mount two brackets on the wall and support a shelf on them. This can also be done if you have a fireplace with no surround.

The wall above the mantelpiece is usually treated as part of the fireplace. In fact, period fireplaces have often included an overmantel as part of the fireplace surround, giving the fireplace even more prominence in an interior. For a similar effect, you could affix rectangular frames made from strips of molding; they should be the same width as the mantel itself. Another approach is to integrate the wooden surround with paneling on the walls—a practice that was common in Colonial houses.

Wall sconces on the wall above the fireplace are often used, but remember that the wiring for these, if new, must be buried in the plaster prior to decorating. If it is impractical to do this, or if you prefer candlelight, you could use candle sconces instead.

A large mirror or a painting or group of pictures is often hung above a fireplace. The frame is normally centered above the mantel, but an eye-catching effect can be produced by hanging it off-center, and balancing this with something tall, such as candlesticks with shades, standing on the mantelshelf.

Apart from the fire itself, the other focal point on a fireplace is the mantelshelf display. Despite the fact that this is a relatively small area, the scope it offers the decorator is huge, particularly as it is nearly at eye level. Candlesticks, china figurines, bronze sculptures, obelisks, vases, antique match holders, carriage clocks,

small framed photos, and miniature topiary trees are all appropriate, but "serious" items like these are frequently interspersed with a variety of whimsical objects and personal mementoes, as well as general ephemera such as invitations, greetings cards, postcards, and fresh flowers.

A formal, symmetrical arrangement of items depends upon having matching pairs of each item, but an informal arrangement can look just as good so long as it is balanced and not too chaotic. A collection of objects such as pitchers in similar shapes in a regimented line can also have great impact. (See the Personal Effects chapter for advice on arranging displays.)

An alternative to the fireplace is a freestanding solid-fuel stove, such as a wood-burning stove. It radiates heat in all directions and still provides a focal point (though not a mantelshelf) for the room.

### PRETTY AS A PICTURE

Why not try something different from a painting or mirror hanging on the wall over the fireplace? A contemporary variation is simply to stand one or more pictures on the mantelshelf—make sure that one is large enough to have an impact. An even more modern variation is to use empty frames. Or, instead of a framed picture or mirror, hang a collection, such as plates or shallow baskets, on the wall. Even if the arrangement of the items on the wall and sitting on the mantel is asymmetrical, try to retain an overall balance.

**LEFT:** Here a mix of period styles works well. The ornate stone fireplace is able to compete with the other strong decorative and architectural elements.

# FOCAL POINTS

When you come into a living room, your eye automatically looks for a focal point. The fireplace normally serves this purpose, but if there isn't one, then another focus is needed, around which the main furniture grouping can be arranged. Establishing the focal point is important because it not only provides the cornerstone of the grouping but also gives the eye something pleasing to rest upon. A large room will have at least two furniture groupings (see page 61) and so will need one or more subsidiary focal points. Whatever you decide to put center stage (see below left for ideas), be sure to give it star treatment with strategic lighting, contrasting color, a generous scale, or clever positioning.

Often the television becomes the focal point of a room simply by default, but it is actually possible to

**ABOVE:** A leafy view provides the backdrop and curtains the frame for this single orchid, creating a colorful focus in a living room. Even the pillows point to it.

**RIGHT:** Simple wooden shutters and a pair of lamps placed at the edges of a wall of glass provide a frame that draws the eye toward a stunning view outside.

## STARRING ROLE

Instead of a fireplace, focal points could be:

- **A window with a great view**
- **A low table displaying an intriguing collection**
- **A large, handsome piece of furniture**
- **A beautiful rug on the floor**
- **A tapestry, huge gilt-framed mirror, or large painting**
- **A wall of collectibles such as straw hats**
- **A wall-storage system**

accommodate a television while devising a more attractive focal point. If there is a fireplace, place the television and VCR inside a discreet cupboard nearby—perhaps in an alcove alongside the fireplace. If necessary, the television can be mounted on a sliding section or turntable that allows it to be swung out to a suitable viewing angle. If there is no fireplace, the focal point could perhaps be built-in cupboards and shelves, an armoire, or a media center to house not only the television, DVD recorder or player, and VCR but also sound equipment.

**ABOVE:** A low table with a small group of rustic pitchers, some colorful flowers, and a single dish forms an effective focal point for the main furniture grouping in this room. Similar pitchers are displayed around the room, but all eyes are on the central group.

# FURNITURE GROUPINGS

The size and shape of your room will determine how many furniture groupings you can fit in. However, even if the room is tiny, it's worth trying to fit in a small secondary group—perhaps just a little table and two occasional chairs in a cozy corner. The main grouping should seat no more than about eight people, with the pieces less than eight feet apart. The aim is to create intimate conversation groups and activity areas, which allow easy movement around them.

Each grouping's focal point (see page 58) will help set the group apart, and you can use the position of furniture to define it further. A corner sofa or a sofa positioned across the room, facing the other seating in the group and with its back to the remaining area, forms an effective divider. If too many windows and doors reduce wall space, place seating and occasional furniture away from the walls, perhaps on the diagonal or even in a triangular arrangement. You can then put storage pieces against the walls.

**LEFT:** Even in a very large room, arrange seating in small conversation groups.

**BELOW:** Placing furniture away from the walls creates space for storage pieces.

# ACTIVITY ZONES

Today's living and family rooms are spaces-within-spaces, which have to be arranged creatively if they are to be practical as well as comfortable and attractive. Although the seating area is the principal furniture grouping, these hardworking rooms often host a variety of different activities, particularly in households that include a range of ages. Whether it is a small room where space is at a premium or a large, open-plan great-room, what's important is that the various pieces of furniture work well together within the available space. One of the best ways of insuring that this happens, while at the same time adding visual interest to the

## DIVIDE AND RULE

Try one of these ways of separating an activity zone from the rest of the room:

- **Use a screen that matches your decor in style, whether it is wicker, painted plywood, fabric, or lacquerwork. You could use the side of the screen that is next to the activity area as a bulletin board to display relevant pictures or paperwork.**
- **Open shelving provides a partial barrier, and you can access the shelves from either side.**
- **A large, bushy plant, or a trough containing ivy climbing up trelliswork, will also soften hard edges and add charm and textural interest.**

room, is to create separate activity zones consisting of small clusters of furniture. Therefore, as well as a seating area, there could be one or more separate zones for, say, reading, writing letters and doing paperwork or homework, working on hobbies or crafts, playing board games, using a computer, watching television or a home theater, gazing out of the window, having an intimate chat, playing music, having a snack or cup of coffee, or dining (see page 126). Many zones could fulfill more than one purpose—for example, a work table could be used for homework and hobbies, or a writing desk for paying bills and working at a computer. A couple of chairs at a small table could serve a multitude of purposes, while a drop-leaf table placed against the back of a sofa set across the room could double as a sofa table and as a work table, with lamps serving both areas.

### EFFICIENCY DRIVE

If you are short of space, make every inch of the activity area work for you. In the floor space that a small table takes up, you can pack in drawers both on top of and under the worktop, along with filing boxes and baskets on the floor beneath, and still have room to sit and work.

**ABOVE:** Areas for work and hobbies can still be beautiful. Make a space that will inspire you with color and pattern, and choose materials that complement the general decor.

Many rooms have alcoves or window bays that can be functional, or you may be able to make space around the perimeter by positioning the main seating away from the walls. If necessary, separate the activity zone with some sort of visual barrier and emphasize the change of purpose with an area rug or even with different flooring. Maintain the room's overall identity using one background color for the walls or floor. Include a focal point within each grouping and incorporate appropriate task lighting (see pages 58 and 80).

Check that the room doesn't look lopsided as a result of your "zoning." Using both small- and large-scale items and balancing them with the permanent elements in the room (such as architectural features) will help prevent this. Picture the furnishings in terms of their visual weight, using, say, a large plant to balance a loveseat, or an armoire to balance a piano. Allow for "traffic lanes" around, rather than through, the zones.

**ABOVE:** A well-lit corner is ideal as a music area. Lamps allow the player to read music without shadows in the evenings, and can also be used to link the area decoratively with the rest of the room.

# THE WORK TABLE

### WORKING IN STYLE

A work table has to allow space to work, but it also ought to look decorative. If the tools you use are attractive in themselves, show them off on the tabletop. Otherwise, a few appropriate small props, such as an old manual typewriter, will give the whole work area a stylish look.

### SEEING THE LIGHT

Because most work done at a table requires good light, the best position for a work table in a living room or family room is usually by a window. By taking care not to block the window too much with the items you're using, you can insure that the rest of the room still benefits from the natural light.

# SEATING

Squashy sofas and generous armchairs are synonymous with comfort. Your lifestyle, the number of people in your household, and the size of the room will all determine what pieces you need. If you live alone and like to entertain a lot of guests, for example, you'll want fewer upholstered pieces and more occasional chairs than a family that spends the evenings relaxing in front of television. And, of course, your decor will affect the style of the seating, whether it is classic wing chairs, contemporary modular sofas, antique wooden settles, Shaker rockers, or streamlined leather-and-steel recliners. Matching sets are out of date (which means that seating can be replaced gradually

**BELOW:** Lots of upholstered pieces give this room a wonderfully comfortable feel, and offer various seating options. The family cat has chosen the warmest seat in the house on which to sleep.

## SEATING IDEAS

Add versatility to your seating with these ideas:

- **An ottoman can act as a footstool, coffee table, or seat. If you use it as a divider between two furniture groupings, people sitting on it can face either way. Some ottomans also provide storage inside.**
- **A fender in front of the fire looks like a decorative part of the fireplace but also provides somewhere for people to perch.**
- **A cushion the same size as a low table can be placed on top of it to transform the table into somewhere to sit.**
- **For family and guests who enjoy lounging on the floor, floor pillows are a good idea.**

**BELOW:** A long, narrow stool like this needlepoint-covered example can be used in front of the fire to provide extra seating or serve as an improvised table.

rather than all at once), but each piece should look an integral part of the whole. Choose upholstery fabrics carefully (see pages 34–7 for advice on combining patterns), and follow your instincts as to what pieces look nice together. Antique and modern furniture, for example, can be combined very successfully. Grouping disparate chairs in front of a unifying shape, such as a curtain, tapestry, or screen, will help draw them together.

Arrange the heavier pieces first and then mass the lighter-weight occasional furniture to balance them. If the room is large, substantial pieces are essential so that they won't look lost. Large-scale seating is also preferable in a small room, making it look more spacious; the secret of this "overscaling" is to use just a few pieces, and not to allow the room to become cluttered.

# TABLES

Apart from seating, the principal furniture in a living room or family room is an assortment of tables. Ideally somewhere to put a drink or a cup of coffee should be within reach of every seat. This could be a coffee table in the center of a furniture grouping, end tables flanking a sofa, a small table between a pair of chairs, or a pier table between two windows. Small chests of drawers, old trunks, stacks of vintage suitcases, glass-topped baskets, and trays (wooden, tole, or papier mâché) on faux bamboo legs are also suitable.

These flat surfaces offer good opportunities for displaying decorative items (see the Personal Effects chapter), but make sure you have left enough space for drinks. When tables are next to sofas or armchairs, they should be roughly the same height as the arms. Tables placed behind sofas should be no higher than the back.

There is no need to buy sets of tables—they look more interesting if they are different, so long as they are compatible with your decor and with each other. (Designers will even split a matching pair, placing the two tables against different walls, to avoid having them on the same wall or at either end of a sofa.) However, a nest of stacking tables can come in handy when you are entertaining.

Tables come in all shapes and sizes, with or without shelves and drawers, and in all styles, from antique to ultra-modern. A low glass coffee table can be useful in a small

**LEFT:** An elegant sofa table, placed in front of a mirror between two windows, is treated like a pier table. The tables in this room are very different in style, but they exist in harmony with each other without dominating the space.

room, as it appears to take up less space than it actually does. Make sure that wooden tables go with the other wood in the room—beech and pine, for example, don't look right with mahogany or walnut but usually are fine with oak. Distressed painted wood fits in well with most materials.

Although a floor-length cloth covering a round table may look a little out of date, a piece of vintage textile can look fabulous draped over a table, with the table legs either left visible or puddling onto the floor.

# GOING BY THE BOOK

Books personalize an interior and make it more inviting, so it's worth fitting proper bookcases in a living room or family room:

- **Alcoves flanking a fireplace are tailor-made for built-in floor-to-ceiling bookcases. Varying the distance between the shelves will allow you to store books of different heights with maximum efficiency.**

- **Stacking some books looks more interesting than standing them all up, and allows you to fit in books that are too tall for the shelves.**
- **A comfortable chair in front of a bookcase in a corner of a room provides a cozy reading spot.**
- **Bookcases can be built on either side of a window, linked by a window seat.**

# BOOKCASES & STORAGE

Good storage systems add to a room's appearance as well as to its practicality. Large pieces of case furniture such as highboys, display cabinets, armoires, bookcases, and bureau-bookcases add height and scale to rooms and make excellent focal points. Designers like to use them to make small rooms look bigger, but care must be taken when "overscaling" in this way to balance the pieces using other large items, such as architectural features, large plants, or paintings—otherwise they can dwarf everything else. Also, don't use a lot of these large pieces in a single room or the effect will be overbearing and ponderous.

Built-in shelves or cupboards will suit many types of decor, from period style to contemporary. Units with cupboards beneath and shelves on top fit beautifully into alcoves and can then be used for display as well as storage. An alternative to visible shelving is to line an alcove with shelves and then fit bifold louver doors or perhaps a blind or shade in front of the shelves. Be aware, however, that alcoves often add individuality to a room and you may lose some of this by filling them.

Instead of built-ins or case furniture, you may prefer readymade modular storage units, which can be arranged in a variety of configurations, from sleek low-level shelves to a wall of storage incorporating a home entertainment center.

Small-scale storage is important, too. In a room with traditional decor, an ottoman with a file cabinet inside would deal with home office paperwork. In a more rustic interior, you could stash a multitude of odds and ends in large baskets, Shaker boxes, band boxes, or even a pie safe.

**RIGHT:** An armoire offers excellent storage for anything from board games to a computer workstation, and does not look at all out of place in a living room or family room. Band boxes stacked on top offer further storage while adding interest at ceiling height.

**ABOVE LEFT:** A slipcover cut to fit around the attractively curved, exposed wooden arms of this chair hangs gracefully to the floor.

**ABOVE RIGHT:** The bold stripes of this cover make a curve-backed easy chair with its fat box cushion and perky pleated valance a striking focal point.

**LEFT:** A squashy, scroll-arm sofa is gently enveloped in a small floral print.

# UNDER COVER

Here are just some of the items that can be slipcovered:

- **Bed headboard**
- **Director's chair**
- **Martha Washington chair**
- **Wing chair**
- **Scroll-arm sofa**
- **Club armchair**
- **Wooden kitchen chair**
- **Folding chair**
- **Wicker chair**
- **Footstool**
- **Slatted garden chair**
- **Table**
- **Twin bed**

# SLIPCOVERS

For centuries people have protected expensive upholstery with cotton or linen slipcovers that were removed only for very special occasions. As a result, the covers' decorative value has grown to the point that it is now as important as their functional aspect. Slipcovers are still used to protect expensive damask and brocade, and they are quick and easy to slip off when necessary. However, today they are made from such colorful and beautiful fabrics that well-made slipcovers look as attractive as the chairs underneath, if not more so, and some are constructed in such a way that you would think they were upholstered in place. As a result, they are now often used to give a worn-out, faded, or jaded chair or sofa a new lease on life, changing its look dramatically. They can add flashes of color or pattern, or a note of whimsy, to a room, perking up the decor with their presence, and because they are removable, they are easy to launder or dry clean. Many people have one set for summer and another for winter; or one set in use and a second set in the wash.

Most chairs and sofas are suitable for slipcovering, apart from those that are not structurally sound. However, velvet, leather, and plastic upholstery do not take to being covered. The best fabrics to use for the cover are firm and closely woven; very thick or heavily textured materials are not suitable. Chintz can be used but is not as durable.

**BELOW LEFT:** Matching stretchy covers cling to a set of fat wicker chairs.

**BELOW:** This tailored slipcover could hardly be simpler in style, with a monogram providing the only decoration.

## COVER NOTES

Slipcovers today are used less for protective purposes and more for their decorative value:

- **Dining chairs can be covered in alternating fabrics or each in a different colorway of one fabric.**
- **A disparate or unattractive group of chairs can be unified by a matching set of covers.**

# PILLOWS & THROWS

Pillows and throws have a practical purpose—to make chairs and sofas more inviting and comfortable—but their decorative value is even greater. They offer tremendous scope for jazzing up your decor, introducing splashes of color, rich pattern, and texture. If one doesn't look right, it is relatively easy to alter, so you can throw caution to the wind and experiment with dramatic fabrics and designs. Remember, though, that these accessories are meant to function as visual punctuation—if you use too many, they lose their impact and just get in the way. Also, be careful not to arrange them too precisely, or people will be afraid to move them into a comfortable position, which would defeat their whole purpose.

Because pillows are so small, you could make them from antique textiles that are not big enough for anything else, or from a wonderful fabric that would be too expensive to use for upholstery or window treatments. You could even base your entire room scheme around that fabric. Conversely, if you want to give the room a lift without changing much, new pillows could make all the difference, accenting colors

## DETAILED LOOK

It's details like these that add interest to a pillow:

- **Buttons, grommets laced with ribbon, or ties can turn ordinary closures into a feature.**
- **Ruffles, pleated flanges, scallops, or zigzag edges can be added in matching or contrasting fabrics.**
- **A striped border with adjacent edges at right angles to each other and mitered corners looks dramatic.**

**LEFT:** A flanged pillow is decorated with appliquéd leaves and fabric roses. Similar roses are available readymade from some notions departments.

**RIGHT:** As well as the traditional piping and cord, you can customize your pillows with bobble or chenille fringes, braids of all widths, ribbons, tassels, crochet lace edging (perfect with gingham), and even feathers, as shown here.

**LEFT:** An inexpensive store-bought pillow cover can be decorated to complement the other textiles in the room. Here, check ribbon is threaded through grommets and tied at the bottom for a feminine look.

**RIGHT:** In a neutral, restrained color scheme, appliqué and machine embroidery can provide interest through texture.

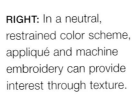

that were otherwise unnoticeable, pulling together disparate colors, or providing new and dramatic contrasts.

Virtually any fabric can be used, including fabric printed with a large graphic design, suede, silk, fake animal skin, petit-point, and delicate embroidered or beaded material. You can, of course, also use the same fabric as for the chair or sofa.

Often the simplest pillows are the most striking, but if you enjoy sewing (or know someone who does), there is plenty of scope for making heirloom-quality pillow covers. For example, a silk or velvet patchwork cover edged with metallic ribbon looks stunning. Solid-color fabric can be decorated with hand or machine embroidery, or large fabric motifs can be appliquéd onto it. A velvet cover will set off a strip of antique needlepoint to perfection.

A throw is a useful device for adding color to a sofa or chair to whatever degree you want. It could be a tribal kilim laid over the back and seat of a solid-color sofa; a wool or antique paisley shawl draped over the back of a loveseat; a cashmere blanket with satin trim, or a tartan blanket, hanging over the arm of an easy chair. A throw that covers an entire sofa will effectively hide worn upholstery, and is made by simply stitching lengths of decorator fabric together and binding the edges. Double-layer throws look nice and can combine two colors, or two patterns, or even two fabrics. Another way of combining fabrics is to add a contrasting border or inset panel to a throw—such as a slub silk border with brushed cotton or chenille.

**LEFT:** Bold, bright fabrics used for pillows and a throw enliven a soft yellow and cream scheme, echoing the colors found on the carpet, lamp base, and little china box. Although they make a dramatic impact, the textiles could be changed easily and for very little expense if required.

**RIGHT:** A pillow and throw in luxurious soft fabrics and rich colors make a cozy corner even more inviting on a cool evening.

# RADIATORS

Most homes have radiators to keep the home cozy year-round, but because modern radiators are not attractive, you may want to replace them with a less visible form of heating. If you live in a historic house, you could fit old cast-iron radiators, which have a dignity, solidity, and sculptural quality that makes them quite pleasing to look at. They can look good with a shelf or length of marble over the top, resting on console-style legs, leaving the radiator visible from the front. They are available from salvage companies, but bear in mind that they are not as efficient as modern versions.

Another possibility is to buy really stylish modern radiators, which come in a variety of striking designs. They can be planned into a room very successfully and, in fact, have become so sculptural in appearance that they are treated practically as works of art.

Nevertheless, the common-or-garden variety is not so attractive, and it always seems to be positioned right where it is most intrusive—especially beneath the window. This creates a problem because long curtains would cover up the radiator and prevent it from warming the room. If you want to use long curtains, the best solution is to keep them tied back and rely on a shade or blind.

Concealing a radiator is another way of dealing with it, either by painting it the same color as the wall behind it, or by boxing it in. A radiator cover can be custom-made to suit your home exactly, with moldings and beading that echo those found elsewhere in the home. Many covers are also available readymade. They generally have a mesh of some sort—wire, cane, metal, wooden lattice—at the front and a shelf above, on which objects can be displayed in the same way as on a mantelpiece. It's important to leave space inside the cover for the air to circulate. Similar designs can be used over radiators beneath windows, and by making it a bit deeper than necessary, the cover can be turned into a window seat. If the window is considerably higher than the seat, the gap could be bridged by building a back to the window seat.

## RADIATING STYLE

Take a look at the style of modern radiators. Some are so striking that we are being forced to reconsider our negative attitudes toward radiators:

- **Some are shaped like long, low, flat panels.**
- **Others resemble black tubes that run along the baseboard, crisply defining the shape of the room.**
- **Many are vertical, including designs shaped like an elongated "X," or in vertical or horizontal slats.**

**RIGHT:** A radiator cover beneath this large window is deep enough to form a proper window seat. The seat helps to make the window an attractive focal point—which the bare radiator is unlikely to have done.

# LIGHTING

**FAR RIGHT:** Chandeliers can work within modern-style rooms as well as traditional ones. This striking candle and glass chandelier adds a dramatic splash of color but is still delicate and sparkly.

**BELOW:** A grand lighting centerpiece provides a wash of ambient light, while a small table lamp offers intimate task lighting.

Lighting can make or break your interior design, determining not only how safe and efficient your home is but also what atmosphere predominates at any given moment. If you are remodeling or building a new home, you can install wiring for wall lights exactly where you want them, floor outlets in the center of a large room, or perhaps even a computerized lighting system that allows you to change the mood at the touch of a button. If you are not remodeling, your options may be more limited. Even so, you can improve your lighting dramatically with the clever use of lamps, dimmer switches, and a variety of light fixtures.

Three basic types of lighting are needed in the living room or family room: general or "ambient" background lighting; task lighting for reading, writing, etc; and accent lighting to emphasize architectural features, focal points, displays, alcoves, or specific areas. The aim is not to create a dazzling overall brightness, but a comfortable level of general illumination, with brighter localized areas and no gloomy corners.

Various light fixtures can provide each type of lighting, and some fixtures are suitable for two or even all three purposes. For maximum flexibility and visual interest, more than one type should be used in a room. Downlights (recessed or surface-mounted) and track lighting can be used for general illumination when fitted with floodlight (wide-beam) bulbs, or for either task or accent lighting when fitted with spotlight (narrow-beam) bulbs. A wallwasher, mounted on the ceiling or recessed into it, "washes" a wall with light, providing general illumination without glare if carefully angled.

## LAMP LIGHT

With their intimate pools of soft light, table lamps are the perfect light source, so be sure to make the most of them:

- **Dot lamps around the room, choosing bases and shades in a variety of shapes and materials.**
- **Even two lamps flanking a sofa don't have to match, so long as they have a similar feeling and "visual weight," and the bottoms of the shades are at the eye level of someone seated.**

It works best if the wall is white or light in color. Uplights bounce light off the ceiling (which, again, is preferably white or light in color), providing a soft background light; or if hidden behind large architectural plants or furniture, they create dramatic accent lighting. Uplights can be freestanding (either small or tall) or wall-mounted.

These fixtures are available in styles ranging from period to cutting-edge, as are wall lights and lamps, which combine effectively with them. Wall lights provide a subtle background light, while table and floor lamps are used for task lighting and also contribute to the background light. The light from central ceiling light fixtures has a notoriously dull, flattening effect. Nevertheless, chandeliers can look fantastic because they incorporate many small lights (see page 119). Lanterns, pendant bowls, and funky modern pendants (see pages 244, 191, and 108) can also work well for dramatic looks.

In most types of light fixtures, either regular tungsten or low-voltage halogen bulbs can be used. Halogen is whiter and more sparkling than tungsten light, which has a warm, yellowish bias. Whatever types of light fixtures and bulbs you settle on, be sure to install dimmer switches for maximum flexibility.

**LEFT:** Lamps are a useful decorative accessory even when switched off, as they add height to an arrangement on a table. Contrasting textures such as a glass base and fabric shade add further interest.

**LIGHT READING**
Siting an armchair by a window insures good natural light for reading in the daytime. An extendable swing-arm wall light mounted on the wall or on a convenient mantelpiece or bookcase supplements the daylight and provides light for reading at night. Ideally, it should be positioned just behind the shoulder of the person seated, so that the light falls on the open book.

**LEFT:** Ultra-modern lamps and light fixtures can look striking with traditional furnishings and antiques, creating an eclectic effect that may be more interesting than conventional period styles.

# MIRRORS

Used creatively, mirrors contribute a great deal to interior decor. A mirror placed near a window will amplify the incoming daylight. At night it will add sparkle and glamour to the room by reflecting candlelight, chandeliers, or other light sources. Well-placed mirrors can also create the illusion of extra space. For example, if you have two tall double-hung windows on one wall, you could line the area between them with mirrored glass as tall as the windows. Frame the mirrored glass with gilt molding, and then hang small paintings on it (hook each to the loop of an adhesive paper plate-hanger which is stuck to the glass). Other visual trickery includes affixing mirrored glass to an entire door or behind shelves in an alcove.

Not only do mirrors make rooms look larger by creating imaginary vistas, but oversize mirrors in substantial frames will make small rooms look bigger. A flamboyant, ornate frame will look right whether the room is period style or modern. Augment the traditional large central mirror over a mantelpiece with a pair of long, narrow ones on either side; or you could hang a painting in the center, and flank the whole fireplace with two floor-to-ceiling framed mirrors.

**LEFT:** Mirrors will make your rooms look bigger and brighter and decorative frames make mirrors into works of art in their own right.

**RIGHT:** This stunning staircase deserves to be seen from every angle. A generous mirror makes the most of this asset.

# SCULPTURES & PAINTINGS

The art you put in your living room or family room makes a strong personal statement. Don't be intimidated or inhibited by the "arty" aspect. This is simply an opportunity to surround yourself with pictures, sculptures, or other objects you love.

Sculptures have traditionally been made by carving a hard material (usually stone or wood), or by casting plaster or metal (particularly bronze) after modeling the sculpture in clay and making a mold. However, modern sculptures are also produced in man-made materials such as resin, aluminum, or steel. In addition, copies of antique museum pieces are available for a fraction of the originals' value, and ceramic figurines can be treated in much the same way as sculptures—which means that there is a great deal of choice within the area broadly known as sculpture.

Apart from very large examples, most sculptures will look better on a table, mantelpiece, desk, column, or plinth. Choose a style appropriate to both the sculpture and your decorating style. For example, in a Federal or American Empire style of room, a classical bust could sit on a low column of stone, marble, or marbleized wood, while in a contemporary interior a piece of primitive art or an abstract sculpture could be placed on a plexiglas plinth.

When siting large sculptures and paintings (or textile wall hangings), keep in mind the position of the room's architectural features and big pieces of furniture so that they balance each other. Also, a large picture needs to be in a spot where there is enough room for people to stand back and look at it properly.

Small pictures look good in small spaces. If these are hung in vertical lines—perhaps flanking a doorway— you could link them by alternating round and rectangular frames or by hanging each line of pictures on a ribbon. In larger spaces, little pictures will have more impact if hung in groups. Ideally some decorative motif should link them, whether it is the medium, colors, mats, frames, artist, or subject matter. However, a uniform group is in danger of looking monotonous, so you might wish to introduce an element of surprise, such as a single oil painting among watercolors, or different-colored mats. See pages 228–9 for advice on arranging picture groups.

**LEFT:** An ornate antique table is used as a "pedestal" for a charming sculpture. The lamp base echoes the color of the sculpture.

# IN GOOD FORM

Add personality to your home with any of the following original and reproduction art objects:

- **Figurative sculpture in bronze or in resin with a bronze finish**
- **Plaster or marble bust of a figure from history or mythology**
- **Alabaster and resin reproduction of classical statue**
- **Miniature Greek statue in alabaster or Parian ware (a nineteenth-century porcelain resembling white marble)**
- **Polished black reconstituted stone reproduction of Art Deco animal sculpture**
- **Staffordshire or other porcelain figurine**
- **Colored resin cast of ancient Greek bust**
- **Copper, tin, or wood folk-art weather vane**
- **African carved wood figure**
- **Modern abstract sculpture in plexiglas, steel, or wood**

### GOOD COMPANIONS

Sculptural folk art will add interest, whatever the decor. This cut-out and painted wooden dummy board would originally have been placed in front of a fireplace in the summer and used as an amusing decorative addition in the winter. It could fulfill this function today, as could a ship's figurehead or an old trade-sign shop figure, such as a bookstore's bust of an author, a wigmaker's mannequin head, a butcher's pig or cow, or a restaurant's standing-chef menu board.

**LEFT:** Here, a collection of paintings has been used to frame the generous fireplace, the door, and the window in this country home. This creates a balanced arrangement of pictures around a core—in this case architectural features.

A rough rule of thumb is that pictures should hang at eye level, but there will be exceptions. Where some people will be standing and others seated, the pictures can be halfway between the two eye levels. Sometimes the position of other large elements in the room will mean that a picture looks better higher or lower than eye level. In a room with a high ceiling, the space above a door can provide an excellent site for a picture that does not need to be viewed from close range. The bottom of a painting hanging above a sofa should be no more than about 14 inches above the sofa back, to prevent the picture from looking isolated; however, it shouldn't be so low that it will get knocked.

If you are redecorating, you could use a painting as the basis for the new color scheme. If you don't plan to redecorate, select pictures that harmonize with your existing decor, or opt for black-and-white or sepia prints or photographs, which will match any color scheme.

## IN THE FRAME

Oil paintings and watercolors are reliable favorites but consider some of the following alternatives, any of which look striking in frames:

- **Family photographs**
- **Botanical or sporting prints**
- **Political cartoons**
- **Period fashion plates**
- **Old maps**
- **Architectural prints**
- **Plaster or bas-relief plaques**
- **Miniatures**
- **Silhouettes**
- **Embroidered samplers**
- **Antique textiles such as lace collars**
- **Appliqué or patchwork wall hangings**

**LEFT:** As well as hanging on the walls, pictures can be hung over mirrors or stood on a mantelpiece. Using colored cord to hang a selection of pictures from a crown molding or picture rail not only adds decorative interest but also links them.

The kitchen and dining room are where family and friends gather to prepare food, share meals, hold full-scale dinner-parties, or simply have a cup of coffee. The kitchen in particular needs to be practical and well equipped, but any dining area should be cheerful and convivial, offering a functional yet stylish setting. A sun porch or other "outdoor room" is also a great meeting place, where the boundaries between indoors and out are blurred.

# MEETING PLACES

# KITCHENS

At the heart of every home is the kitchen, whether you have a spacious country-style room or a more compact food-preparation area. Designing and creating a new kitchen area is one of the most dramatic, and often costly, transformations you can make to your home, so it is vital to do your homework before you call in the designers and builders. It may, in fact, be possible to produce a dramatic makeover without too much upheaval or expense. From traditional rustic havens to sleek, minimal spaces the choice for the modern kitchen is seemingly endless, but armed with some inspiration and a little knowledge you can create the perfect room for your home.

**RIGHT:** Generous storage, display, and counter space insure that this spacious kitchen is a delight to use and a pleasure to be in.

# KITCHEN COLORS

The colors of cabinets, tiles, walls, floors, appliances, and furniture all play a part in a kitchen color scheme, and it may not be feasible to change many of these. Therefore, decide what fixtures have to remain, and use this information as the basis of your decor. (Keep in mind that walls are relatively simple to paint, and updating cabinets and tiles may be easier than you think—see pages 96, 99, and 197.) If you are completely remodeling, a collection of pottery, a set of storage jars, a favorite picture, or the fabric you will have at the windows could serve as your thematic starting point.

Soft, muted colors are ideal in a kitchen, because they make it seem calmer and more spacious. White (or, for a lovely old-fashioned look, cream) maximizes available light and looks clean and pristine. A darker floor or cabinets add tonal depth, while colorful accents prevent white from being too glaring or clinical, and light colors from being too bland. Avoid having too many accents in the same color or the look may seem contrived, but by the same token, try to avoid a fragmented effect. Kitchens offer plenty of scope for striking a happy medium—for example, a bowl of tomatoes, apples, or lemons could echo the colors of a cookie jar or dish towel, while a wicker pot stand could showcase enamel or cast-iron pans in your chosen hues.

**BELOW:** Sunny yellows and reds work well with the warm tones of the natural wood to make a kitchen that feels cozy and inviting.

**RIGHT:** The bright blue range was the starting point for this cheery kitchen. Blue and red accessories enliven the white cabinets and give a delightful, retro feel.

## GOOD MIXERS

- **White with an accent of cobalt blue (which was used in kitchens for centuries as a deterrent to flies) is a classic mix for the kitchen.**
- **Soft green—mint, pistachio, celadon, or a light lime—teamed with white, and perhaps sky blue and a dash of red, works well in the kitchen.**
- **Yellow looks good with white or gray, and also with splashes of bright red, while light yellow goes well with soft blue-gray, sky blue, or navy.**
- **A combination of strong red, yellow, and blue can be overpowering in large doses but these colors make perfect accents in a white kitchen with natural wood cabinets.**

# KITCHEN CABINETS

Personalizing your kitchen cabinets can involve anything from buying new knobs to replacing all the cabinetry. If you are buying new cabinets, you can choose from a wide range of materials, including solid woods (such as pine, oak, teak, maple, or black walnut), birch-faced plywood, beech or wenge veneer, stainless steel, and aluminum. Combinations of contrasting materials such as wood and stainless steel are also possible and can look very striking. The choice of styles is equally enormous, ranging from simple, countrified "Shaker" to cutting-edge modern.

When choosing, take into account not just the cabinets' appearance and how they will look with your appliances, but also their practicality. The countertop and backsplashes you plan to use (see page 106) need to be considered, too. Decide whether you want to hide everything behind closed doors or combine cabinets with open storage (see page 100), whether you need any tall cabinets for brooms and mops, how many drawers you'll need, and whether you want to hide your refrigerator and dishwasher behind panels that match the cabinets. Consider how to personalize the interiors of the cabinets, too—do you want corner carousels, door-mounted racks, slide-out wicker baskets, deep drawers for pans, a pull-out ironing board, slots for trays, baking pans, and chopping boards, or perhaps an appliance "garage" for small, countertop appliances? Finally, think about the layout. It's important to create separate zones for food storage, food preparation, cooking, and clearing up, with sinks, appliances, work space, and appropriate storage for each activity all within reach.

If your cabinets are looking dated but are structurally sound and you are happy with the layout of your kitchen, you could consider just replacing the doors, drawer fronts, and end panels (and perhaps the countertop—see page 106). Another possibility is to replace the doors with curtains. Alternatively, if the existing doors have recessed panels, you could cut out the panels and replace them with curtains, punched tin, or glass and chickenwire. Painting or staining existing cabinets will create a whole new effect at a fraction of the price of replacement (see page 99). Finally, a simple option that has a surprisingly dramatic effect is to replace the knobs on the doors and the drawer pulls.

**GLAZED LOOKS**
Wall-hung kitchen cabinets with glass doors look really nice—if what's inside is neatly arranged and interesting. Using a bright wallpaper or paint, or lighting, inside the cabinets will help compensate for colorless contents, but having both glass doors and solid doors will give more flexibility in your storage.

**RIGHT:** Fabric curtains make charming "doors" for kitchen cabinets, and tie in with the rustic look of the room.

# PAINT MAGIC

If your existing cabinets are solid wood, laminate, or medium-density fiberboard, painting them will create a whole new look. Try one of these ideas:

- **Painting dark cabinets a pale color will make your kitchen look lighter and airier.**
- **Painting adjacent doors and drawers in alternating colors, or even in a range of different colors, can look good, if you use muted, flat shades to prevent them from looking childish.**
- **Paint one or more doors with black latex chalkboard paint, on which you can write shopping lists or messages with chalk.**
- **Before painting, the surface must be thoroughly prepared by sanding down, cleaning, and priming, particularly if it is laminate.**
- **For wooden cabinets, stripping them down and then staining them rather than painting them will allow the grain to show through.**

# OPEN STORAGE

Whether a kitchen has built-in or freestanding cabinets, there is a need for open storage as well. It adds variety and provides excellent display space. Even if you are not remodeling your kitchen, there is probably a spot that would benefit from adding some form of open storage. Open shelving is the most common and versatile type, used for everything from delicate glassware to huge pots and pans. Individual wooden bracket shelves, perhaps incorporating a peg rail or small drawers, add a country flavor to a kitchen, while "floating" glass shelves with no visible means of support look dramatic in a modern kitchen. Open shelving sandwiched between wall-hung cabinets prevents them from looking oppressive, and a built-in plate-draining rack above the sink allows drip-dry storage. Narrow shelves mounted under wall cabinets and over doors and windows provide extra storage in otherwise unused areas.

A wall-mounted rail, or a metal overhead rack suspended from a joist or crossbeam, offers a decorative and handy place to hang pans and utensils using S-hooks. A pegboard or a wire grid can be mounted on a wall near the stove or sink to create another place to hang utensils.

**BELOW:** Open shelving looks equally attractive on the wall or as part of a work island. However, for unattractive items or for little-used things that would just get dusty on open shelves, most kitchens also need some closed-in storage, whether a built-in armoire-style cupboard like the one on the left of this kitchen or regular cabinets.

# SHELF LIFE

### ON THE SHELF

A shelving unit or plate rack mounted on the wall above a base cabinet can be made to resemble an old-fashioned hutch, or the shelves can run from floor to ceiling, bookcase-style. Try to display only items you use regularly, otherwise they will become dust-catchers.

### BASKET CASE

Baskets and hampers placed on shelves or hanging on walls can hold anything from fruit and vegetables to table linen and silverware. Available in all shapes and sizes, they add gorgeous textures to any style of kitchen.

# FREESTANDING STORAGE

It is not surprising that freestanding storage has been increasingly adopted in kitchens: Standalone pieces offer flexibility as well as good looks. Originating from old-fashioned kitchens before the days of streamlined built-in cabinets, freestanding storage was used in country and town alike. The renewed popularity of this type of kitchen can be attributed partly to a nostalgia for the family-oriented lifestyle associated with this time, but there are more pragmatic reasons for its success.

In the first place, if the pieces used are not too small and ad hoc, a kitchen featuring freestanding storage can be both interesting and attractive. Each storage item is an individual piece of furniture, with its own materials, color, and character. Also, freestanding storage usually incorporates open shelving and overhead racks (see pages 100–1), adding to the visual interest.

Depending on the arrangement of the pieces, the furniture can be at least as functional as built-in storage. Many storage pieces offer capacious space for large items like casseroles and soup tureens, which are often awkward to accommodate in conventional cabinets. Because the main work surface is usually a central table or island, rather than a long countertop, you don't have to walk so far back and forth as you prepare food. Small appliances, such as coffeemakers, mixers, and juicers, can be stored on top of any freestanding pieces that aren't too tall. In addition, the different work surfaces are at varying heights, making them more versatile—you can choose the work surface that is the right height for whatever job you are doing. Added advantages: Freestanding storage is relatively inexpensive and can be purchased gradually, and you can take your kitchen with you if you move to a new house. Surely the greatest benefit, however, is the fact that, with the kitchen becoming a family room, freestanding storage is infinitely adaptable to modern needs.

**LEFT:** Because this glass-fronted cupboard would not look out of place in the living area adjacent to the kitchen, it helps to unify the space. However, it still provides practical storage and work space in a family kitchen.

## STANDING ROOM ONLY

Here are some of the storage pieces you could press into service:

- **Hutch**
- **Armoire**
- **Wardrobe**
- **Bookcase**
- **Shop display cabinets**
- **Chest of drawers**
- **Butcher's block cart with built-in storage**
- **Apothecary drawers**
- **Sideboard**

# SMALL KITCHENS

Small does not have to mean cramped. With planning, a compact kitchen can be efficient and a pleasure to work in. To make the space seem as big as possible, aim for a sleek, streamlined look—that means banishing clutter and throwing out all those gadgets you hardly ever use. There's nothing worse when cooking than having to perch everything on a few inches of clear work space.

Good lighting is essential, too (see pages 108–9). If you are replacing your cabinets, bear in mind that shiny, light surfaces will make the room seem larger. Try to create a uniform, unbroken facade, with appliances blending in or hidden behind panels. Open shelving or wall cabinets with glass doors will be less oppressive than wall cabinets with solid doors in a confined space. Paint the walls so they blend in with the cabinets and worktop. It's a good idea to avoid a strongly patterned wall covering if the backsplash is tiled, because the gridlike pattern of the grout could fight with it. You can always use color accents to prevent the scheme from looking bland. Augment your storage space with wall-mounted racks, rails, pegboards, and grids (see page 100).

If possible, continue the kitchen wall color or flooring into the next room. If the door opens inward, consider rehinging it so it opens outward, or replacing it with a folding or sliding door. In fact, removing the door completely and possibly even widening the doorway would make the kitchen look a lot bigger. Could you borrow any space from adjacent rooms, to create a pantry or a laundry cupboard? If you are replacing appliances, would slimline or miniature versions be large enough for your needs? It is even possible to buy an all-in-one mini-kitchen that actually fits into a closet.

**LEFT:** A window or open doorway makes a small room seem more spacious, even if it is the trompe l'oeil variety as shown here.

**ABOVE RIGHT:** Streamlined, built-in cabinets will make a kitchen look bigger, but in this kitchen old-fashioned coziness is the priority.

## UTILIZING EVERY INCH

Consider space-saving ideas like these if you are buying new kitchen cabinets:

- **Wide, shallow drawers behind the kick-plate**
- **Wall cabinets that continue up to the ceiling**
- **Fold-down or pull-out countertops**
- **A shallow cupboard or an extra-deep countertop in one area, for bar stools underneath**
- **Specially designed cabinets for corners**
- **Two shelves instead of one inside each cabinet**
- **Racks or pegboards on the inside of cabinet doors**

# KITCHEN SURFACES

Now that the kitchen has become a living and entertaining area, it needs to be as attractive as it is functional. Yet the surfaces—floor, countertop, backsplash, and cabinetry—have to be impervious to cuts, burns, fumes, grease-laden steam, and splatters. Floors that will survive all this include resilient floorings (rubber, vinyl, linoleum, and cork) laminates and glazed ceramic tiles (see page 196). Stone slabs and tiles, terrazzo, quarry and terra-cotta tiles, and wood are also suitable, provided they are sealed initially and then resealed regularly (see pages 51 and 196). Stone and tiles will feel less cold underfoot if underfloor heating is installed. Sheets of stainless steel and aluminum are used for floors, too, but are very slippery, so are unsuitable for the elderly or families with young children.

Countertop materials have expanded enormously, with choices including laminates, granite, slate, basalt, marble, solid surfacing materials, stainless steel, a variety of woods such as beech and maple, polished concrete in various colors, and toughened glass. Ceramic tiles are sometimes used, but they are prone to crack and the grout discolors. Popular materials for backsplashes include stainless steel, ceramic or glass tiles, stone tiles, plexiglas, and toughened glass.

Cabinets, too, need to be able to resist the onslaught, particularly near the stove. Laminates and stainless steel are the easiest to clean, but in a country-style kitchen, wood (which needs to be well sealed) looks the most appropriate. Often, a combination of more than one material gives the most versatile option, as each can be used in the most suitable place.

**RIGHT:** The mellow natural wood in cabinets, flooring, and countertops, as well as in the chairs and stool, links this country-style kitchen to the leafy view from the windows.

# KITCHEN LIGHTING

Good lighting is more important in the kitchen than anywhere else in the home. The cooks need to be able to see what they are doing—they must not be cutting with sharp knives, pouring boiling water, or slaving over a hot stove in the dark. There are more accidents in the kitchen than anywhere in the home, often because people are working in their own shadows, cast by a central pendant light behind them.

Apart from illuminating the cooks' activity preparing food and cooking it, kitchen lighting should provide good, shadowless task lighting for the other activities, such as washing dishes, filling and emptying the dishwasher, eating, and reading. It should also provide just the right level of background lighting—neither too bright nor too dim.

If the kitchen has wall cabinets, the best task lighting for the countertop is concealed strip lighting hidden by baffles on the underside of the cabinets. The strips can be either fluorescent strips (which give off a rather harsh white light) or tungsten strips (which produce a more yellowish tone). Downlights can also be recessed into the underside of wall cabinets.

For areas where there are no wall cabinets, a line of pendant lights is useful, positioned carefully so that they don't create glare. Pendant lights are available in some fantastic designs which look terrific hanging in an evenly spaced line. Near a stove, however, the design should be simple so that the lighting fixtures don't harbor grease. Also, make sure that they are hanging directly over the work surface. The cooktop will probably have a light above it in the exhaust fan, but if not, then a task light is needed here; and a task light is

**RIGHT:** A pair of low-hanging pendants with chic glass shades are ready to provide task lighting on this work surface when the daylight is no longer streaming in.

also essential over the sink. Track lighting with angled spotlights can be used if they are fitted with crown-silvered bulbs, as these help reduce the glare that spotlights tend to create. Preventing glare is particularly important in the kitchen, because the shiny surfaces will exacerbate any problem with it. A downlight on the ceiling could be good here, too; some types swivel so that you can aim the beam exactly where you need it. Yet another form of task lighting is the shaded spotlight on an adjustable arm, mounted on the wall over the work surface. Ideally, these task lights would be on a separate switch from the general lighting. If the kitchen is used for dining, the lights should be fitted with a dimmer, so that they can be carefully controlled.

The amount of background light required will depend on how much task lighting there is (since some of the task lighting contributes to the overall level of light) and the level of daylight in the room, as well as the wall and ceiling colors. Low-voltage downlights, which have either broad or narrow beams, provide good background lighting. So do wall-mounted halogen uplights, which throw light onto the ceiling (the ceiling must be light-colored) and are high in wattage. More background lighting can come from concealed strip lighting on the tops of the wall cabinets, forming a dramatic ribbon of light running all around the tops of the cabinets.

## IN FOCUS

Accent lighting can add to the atmosphere of a kitchen:

- **Use small accent spots to highlight displays on shelves.**
- **During a meal, allow accent lights to stay on when the other lights are dimmed.**
- **Interior lighting in glass-fronted cabinets allows displays to be seen clearly.**

# COZY CORNERS & NOOKS

The breakfast nook is undoubtedly a lovely invention. This is not the big table where friends or family sit down for a meal, but a small, intimate spot to sit and read a letter or do the crossword. When your next-door neighbor drops in for a cup of coffee, this is where you will gravitate to. If you are lucky enough to have an empty alcove or free corner in your kitchen, it's tailor-made for a proper nook. Even if you don't have anywhere obviously suitable for a nook, you can still create a close approximation.

The ideal position for a nook is in front of a window. If there are already cabinets there, that doesn't matter. Just create the nook in front of them—it is easily moved for access to the cabinets (though it would be a good idea to reserve them for items you don't use every day). The nook is made from two benches placed either side of the window, at right angles to it, creating storage inside both the backs (accessed via cupboard doors in the backs of each bench) and the seats (accessed via hinged tops). Benches can be purchased readymade or you can have a carpenter build them for you. Between the two benches and butting up to the window, place a table that matches the seats. Cover the seats with box cushions.

If there is a corner you can use but no window, you can instead exploit the almost magnetic attraction corner seating can exert. Install a wainscot as the back of the seating extending for about four feet each side of a corner. Against that, position two backless benches, one of them three feet long and the other three feet minus the depth (front to back) of the bench. Put a three-foot-square table in the corner.

## AROUND THE CORNER

Here are some other ways to create a cozy corner:

- **Build a simple triangular table and fit it into an awkward corner, placing two bar stools next to it.**
- **Put two modular sofas in a corner, adding pillows, and place a square table in front of them.**
- **Make your own alcove using two floor-to-ceiling built-in cupboards on adjacent walls near a corner. Build an L-shaped bench between them to fit into the corner, and place a table in front of them.**
- **Tuck an armchair or two and an occasional table into a corner for instant coziness.**

**ABOVE LEFT:** A small table with refreshments next to a window is at the heart of every cozy corner.

**RIGHT:** Comfortable seating tucked into a corner by a window is almost as enticing as a genuine breakfast nook.

# DINING AREAS

Good food and good company deserve the very best setting, whether it's a formal dinner for a special occasion, or just a quiet meal with the family. Choose comfortable and versatile furnishings and lighting that can be adapted to any situation and encourage your guests to relax and enjoy themselves. Dressing the table makes an occasion special and allows you to introduce a fresh look with minimal fuss and expense.

**RIGHT:** This classic, Scandinavian-style dining room has been dressed for a formal dinner, complete with sparkling glass and china, and candles for atmosphere. But the same room could be used for a quiet lunch with friends or a family breakfast—it's all in the detail.

# DINING AREA COLORS

**RIGHT:** The chair fabric and items on the table provide almost the only color accents in this ethereal white dining room. The different pinks make the scheme more interesting than if they all matched exactly.

**BELOW:** A blue and white bowl and gingham chair covers add a cheerful freshness to a white dining area. The black metal chandelier adds a pleasing sharp note to the scheme.

Whether you have a dedicated dining room or a dining area in the kitchen or another room, there is a lot you can do to make it special. The colors that will work best depend upon when the room is used. An eating area in the kitchen, for example, might be used principally in the daytime for relaxed breakfasts, brunches, and lunches with family and friends. In that case, you'll want it to look as light and welcoming as possible. White would be a terrific starting point. You could use it for walls, window treatments, floor, and chairs then add a table in stunning black wenge (a tropical hardwood) or a brown antique pine table and hutch (dresser). Or create a blue and white scheme, which will look crisp and fresh in any style of home. To prevent the white from looking clinical, use lots of soft textures. You could also paint one whole wall in a vibrant color, and echo this in accents such as chair seat upholstery or vases.

Dining areas work best if they are integrated with the rest of the room but also separately defined, and color is a good way of doing this. Use the main color from the other part of the room as an accent in the dining area (for a rug under the table, table linen, glassware, etc), and vice versa. The distinction between the areas needs to be obvious, as subtle differences go unnoticed.

In a dedicated dining room that is used mostly in the evening, you can choose colors that look good by candlelight and artificial light, creating a moody setting and a sense of occasion. Deep red has traditionally been used in dining rooms, and with good reason—used boldly over a large expanse, it looks particularly cozy, warm, and inviting and, in addition, is very flattering to complexions. (It is also said to stimulate both conversation and the appetite.) Other deep, rich colors, such as terra-cotta, deep rose, plum, eggplant (aubergine), chocolate, nutmeg, bottle green, midnight blue, or charcoal will look equally dramatic on walls (though tungsten lighting may make blues and greens look slightly muddy). Highlight these rich hues with plenty of glass, candlelight, and sparkling gold and silver—gold works best with warm colors and silver with cool, but it is perfectly all right to mix these metals together. If the dining room interconnects with another room and the two are used together, say for entertaining, it is a good idea to use color to link the rooms visually, by echoing the colors used in one with accents in the other.

**LEFT:** On a hard floor, color is used to delineate between the eating area around the table, and the general thorough-fare of the room.

# DINING AREA FLOORING

In a dining area, the flooring is like a stage for the table and chairs, so it needs to be appropriate to the decor. Hard flooring, such as wood (see page 51), terra-cotta (unglazed clay), or stone, looks elegant and beautiful. The rustic patina of a well-worn terra-cotta floor looks wonderful in a farmhouse-style room. At the other end of the stylistic scale, marble is the ultimate floor for a formal dining room and is available in a wide range of colors. As well as marble, many other stones, including sandstone, limestone, slate, granite, and terrazzo (stone chips set in a cement base) are also fashionable today for flooring, and many look equally at home in elegant or casual rooms. Available as slabs (flagstones) or tiles, they are not only handsome but also very durable. However, all stone can feel cold underfoot, which is why underfloor heating is often installed beneath it. Although easy to clean, terra-cotta and some types of stone can stain easily and may therefore require regular stripping, cleaning, and refinishing. As a result, many people prefer look-alike ceramic tiles or good-quality vinyl tiles that are designed to resemble them (see page 196). Another problem associated with all forms of hard flooring is that it can be noisy when walked upon, but the use of rugs and other textiles in the room will help to deaden the sound. Rugs will also make it softer underfoot.

**BELOW:** A striking grid pattern has been created in this wood floor by staining wood strips at regular intervals, and then staining stripes of the same width at right angles to them.

Natural matting such as seagrass or sisal is sometimes used in dining areas but is not ideal because it holds crumbs, absorbs liquids, and can be prone to creeping. Wall-to-wall carpet (see pages 188–9) in a medium to heavy-duty quality is suitable, though it is advisable to avoid light colors and treat the carpet with a stain-repellent. Using a different flooring from that found in the rest of the room is a good way to delineate a dining area that is part of a larger space—or you could use a rug over hard flooring.

### CENTER STAGE
By "framing" a dining table, an area rug makes it the center of attention, thereby adding to the sense of occasion. However, a rug can ruck up easily and may not withstand chairs being dragged over it a lot. Choose a hard-wearing one, and make sure it is large enough to allow chairs to be pulled well back from the table. Secure it to the floor with a double-sided tape especially for rugs, or at least use an "anti-creep" underlay.

# LIGHTING DINING AREAS

Dining area lighting has to be both atmospheric and functional. For dinner parties, there is nothing better than the flickering light of candles for creating an intimate and flattering glow at the table. Supplement this with low-level lighting around the walls, in the form of uplights (see page 83) in corners or behind large plants, wall lights, table lamps, or accent lights trained on wall art or sculptures. If you like to serve the food from a sideboard or side table, a downlight (see page 80) directed at it is useful.

Downlights can also be installed in the ceiling above the table, but the positioning is crucial—they should be directed either at the centerpiece or along the length of the table, rather than at the chairs. An alternative to downlights is the overhead pendant, positioned low enough to avoid glare. If the table is fairly long, you could use a line of two or three pendants over it, which will help reduce glare. Star lights set into the ceiling (see page 191) can also look fabulous twinkling above a dining table. Perhaps the most decorative lighting of all, however, is the chandelier.

Separate switches, all fitted with dimmers, are essential, so that you can fine-tune the lighting to suit the occasion. If the dining area is part of a larger room, separate switches and dimmers will allow you to knock back the lights in the unused areas to give the dining table the starring role.

LEFT: Supplement soft candlelight with a glittering chandelier, glowing table lamps, or other atmospheric background lighting.

RIGHT: Choose a bigger chandelier than you think you'll need, as they always look smaller once they are in position.

# DINING TABLES

Wherever your dining area is situated, the table plays the leading role. A vast range of dining tables is available today, from wooden antiques with a wonderful patina to glitzy mirror-top tables, and from painted metal versions in muted shades to funky plastic tables in vivid colors. Many offer dramatic combinations of materials like steel with dark wood, or glass with chrome. When choosing a table, be sure to consider the treatment the surface will receive—a valuable antique may not be a sensible idea if you will be continually having to protect the surface from coffee cups, spilled wine, or your pet's paw prints.

**ABOVE:** A sunny window with a nice view is a lovely spot for a dining table.

**LEFT:** Natural light and an informal table setting can give a breakfast table a completely different look from its dinnertime mode.

## FEEDING A CROWD

Camouflage the following with large tablecloths or sheets the next time you plan a sit-down meal or large buffet for a crowd:

• **A sheet of particleboard (chipboard) laid over a table to enlarge the tabletop**
• **A line of folding card tables of the same size**

The most beautiful tables can carry a high price tag, but, in fact, you can get away with any old table, so long as it's sturdy—just give it a couple of coats of paint or cover it up completely with one or two glamorous cloths. For this reason, if you have a limited budget it is better to spend extra on dining chairs rather than the table itself.

The shape and size of the table will probably be dictated by the proportions of the dining area. If that is long and narrow, then an oblong or elliptical table will make best use of the space. A round table is good in a square room because the shape of the table softens the lines of the room. Allow about four feet all around the table to leave room for people to walk behind those who are seated in chairs, and for chairs to be moved

back. To seat four people in comfort, the table should be at least three feet square, or 42 inches in diameter; for six people, it needs to be at least five feet long and three feet wide, or 51 inches in diameter; and for eight people, it should be 78 x 42 inches, or five feet in diameter.

The table doesn't necessarily have to be placed right in the center of the dining area. Siting it off-center might free up floor space and ease the traffic flow through the room, or you could place it against the wall during the day and move it out to center stage when entertaining guests to dinner. Wherever the table is positioned, don't leave it bare when not in use—a pretty runner down the center or a vase of flowers will make all the difference, or you could create a "tablescape" (a carefully planned arrangement of objects on a tabletop).

**ON A PEDESTAL**
A round table encourages relaxed conversation, and a central pedestal offers more flexibility and comfort because no one has to straddle a table leg.

# DINING CHAIRS

Dining chairs can be a major expense because you usually need at least four and sometimes as many as eight or ten. But because a rickety or uncomfortable set of chairs can completely spoil a meal, it is worth taking some care over them. Of course, it may be that they are perfectly sound and comfortable but not very attractive, or perhaps you are redecorating or changing your dining table, and they just don't look right anymore. In that case, the simplest remedy is to have some slipcovers made for them (see page 73). It doesn't matter whether the chairs are upholstered or not—most chairs (even folding ones) can be slipcovered, and a wide range of styles is possible.

## OTHER HOT SEATS

There's no need to restrict yourself to chairs as the only seating option around a dining table. Here are some other ideas:

- **A high-backed settle, deacon's bench (which has a spindle back and arms), or old church pew provides cozy seating on one side of a table.**
- **A banquette (upholstered bench) is both informal and comfortable. It takes up less space than chairs and can be used for storage if the seat is hinged.**
- **Even a window seat can be called into action if a dining table is placed in front of it.**

If you are buying new dining chairs, you have to decide whether you want the upholstered type. Chairs with upholstered seats and backs are the most expensive, but they are supremely comfortable, allowing you and your guests to linger over your after-dinner coffee in comfort. Traditionally, the two chairs at the head and foot of an oblong table are carvers (with arms), but this is not essential, and obviously isn't appropriate if your table is round or square. Unfortunately, the upholstery attracts stains like a magnet, particularly if used by children, so have the fabric treated with a stain repellent and be prepared to have the chairs re-covered eventually. You could protect the upholstery with slipcovers, which can be laundered. The slipcovers can be removed for special occasions—but you may like them so much that you never bother.

As an alternative to fully upholstered chairs, chairs with upholstered seats and wooden backs are comfortable, and the drop-in seats are very easy to re-cover if you want to change the fabric. Wooden chairs can also have wooden or rush seats. Rush seats are not as hard as wood, but they do tend to collect crumbs. For chairs with no upholstery, you can tie cushions to the seats (and some more to the backs, if you wish).

**LEFT:** Tailored slipcovers are ideal for dressing up dining chairs that have seen better days. Slipcovers can be made in fabrics to match a tablecloth or to suit the time of year.

**RIGHT:** Tie-on cushions make hard chairs more comfortable, and also help protect valuable antiques from wear and tear.

**TAKING THE CHAIR**
Harlequin sets of chairs often have more personality than matching sets, and even just having the carvers different from the others is enough to break the uniformity. Easy chairs can be drawn up to the table and used as carvers, though they are not as upright as dining chairs and the seats are lower.

**LEFT:** Open-back dining chairs are a good choice for small rooms, as they add comfort without taking up as much visual space as chairs with upholstered backs. The backs on these chairs are only just visible above the table top, which also reduces their overall mass.

Harlequin (mismatched) sets create a free-spirited, informal look that is highly fashionable these days. Even if the chairs are all different, they will probably work well together, so long as they are roughly similar in height and shape. Fabric can be used to unify them, if desired, whether in the form of cushions, seat upholstery, or slipcovers. To create the effect of a harlequin set in chairs that are all the same, you could vary the fabric—using different colors of one type of material, or the same color but checks on some and stripes on others.

Just as chairs don't have to match each other, so they don't have to match the table. A combination of different materials, such as wood with metal, or metal with marble, may even work better than matching materials, depending on your decor.

# FLEXIBLE DINING

As family meals and entertaining become more informal, dual-purpose dining rooms are increasingly common. Part of the kitchen, family room, living room, sun porch, or even foyer may serve as a dining area, or a dining room can double as a den, study, library, playroom, guest bedroom, or studio.

The secret is to make the dining table dual-purpose (see box, right). If you want also to minimize the space it takes up, choose a convertible table, which flips open and folds out to double or triple its size. Or place two matching semicircular or narrow rectangular tables against the wall, pushing them together for meals. Dining chairs can be dispersed around the home (with slipcovers to match each room)—or use folding or stacking chairs. If the dining room is doubling as a den or guest bedroom, you will also need a sofa-bed or a couple of armchairs, plus a small table which, in turn, could be used for serving food when you are dining in the room. If you are separating the dining area from the rest of the room, a low cupboard topped with narrow shelving could be used for storage and a serving area.

## TOP TABLES

A dining table can take on any number of dual functions, according to the room the dining area shares:

- **Kitchen: prepping station**
- **Family room or playroom: games or crafts table**
- **Foyer or library: library table**
- **Study or studio: work table**
- **Living room: display or cocktail table**
- **Sun porch: plant table**
- **Guest room: hobby table**

**LEFT:** If a table is to be dual-purpose, make sure the surface will withstand whatever it is subjected to. You can always cover it with a pretty tablecloth for meals.

**RIGHT:** In the center of a foyer, a round library table used for books and papers or as a display area by day can quickly morph into a dining table at night. The lights are dimmed, and chairs discreetly scattered around the room are drawn up to become dining chairs.

# DINING AREA STORAGE

**LEFT:** A sideboard provides good storage space along with a place for such dining-room essentials as a bowl of fruit, flowers, decanters, a table lamp, and a soup tureen.

**BELOW:** Though not originally designed for dining rooms, a handsome chest of drawers does not look out of place and provides storage for silverware and table linens.

**BELOW RIGHT:** A shallow cabinet fits neatly into even the smallest dining area, adding visual interest as well as shelf space for dinnerware and a narrow serving area.

To be functional, a dining area has to have not just a table and chairs but also reasonable storage, so that china, silver, glassware, table linen, and other dining accoutrements will be at hand. Built-in cabinets and shelving are particularly good, as they make excellent use of space and are very decorative. You could build them around a window and window seat, with cupboards to hold the basics, and shelving on top for the most attractive items and perhaps also some books—which make a very cozy backdrop for dining.

Try to include one or two tall pieces such as a china cabinet or a hutch (dresser)—both of which offer display space, too—or an armoire. A corner cupboard is marvelous, as it not only uses dead space but also looks cozy and welcoming, drawing you into the room when placed opposite a door. Low pieces like a sideboard, chest of drawers, or pie safe can double as serving areas, and paintings or wall hangings can be placed over them to balance the taller pieces. Although these are all traditional items found in both antique and reproduction versions, contemporary pieces are also available and can look stunning with other modern furniture or juxtaposed with antiques.

# EATING IN SPLENDOR

One of the great pleasures of entertaining is creating a gorgeous table. There is no doubt that a beautifully set table turns a dinner party into a special occasion. It doesn't need to be grand, and it doesn't have to be in a separate room—the important thing is that it is inviting and full of atmosphere.

The table, resplendent in all its glory, is the focal point of the dining area. Candles in floral arrangements, candlesticks, candelabras, girandoles (wall sconces with mirror backing), or even a chandelier, create an unbeatable atmosphere. Warm and inviting, candlelight is flattering to skin tones and adds sheer romance to the table as the flickering flames are reflected in crystal, silver, and gleaming china. They are an essential for any special gathering but are so evocative that it's nice to use them at every dinner.

## PUTTING ON THE STYLE

For a glamorous table setting, try some of these ideas:

- **Rather than a plain tablecloth, use a vintage paisley shawl, a Moroccan silk bedspread, an Indonesian silk ikat (a cloth woven from tie-dyed threads), or a patchwork quilt.**
- **Make napkin rings from grosgrain ribbon or a circle of ivy.**
- **Layer the china—as each plate is removed, the next is revealed, finishing with a silver, brass, pewter, glass, or china charger (underplate).**

**ABOVE:** Taking care over the table setting will make breakfast or teatime special too. A crisp lace tablecloth and a classic silver tea or coffee set will make even the simplest meal into a real occasion.

Choose wonderful table linen to create the backdrop for your setting. Crisp, white damask is traditional for formal dinners, but there is a massive choice of other possibilities, both formal and informal, including plain linen with delicate cutwork edging or other embroidered decoration. Modern versions are available but vintage textiles look much more romantic. An openwork or lace cloth allows the table to show through, as do placemats (unless laid over an undercloth), so make sure the table surface is worthy of the attention.

**RIGHT:** This formal table setting is all about sparkle, from the glassware to the edges of the china and even the stylish silver cutlery. Use fresh flowers and your best table linen—immaculately pressed—to create a dramatic first impression when your guests sit down to dinner.

# OUTDOOR ROOMS

Outdoor rooms offer the best of both nature and the indoors. By bringing the garden inside, or taking the comforts of home outside, they help to blur the boundaries between the two zones. When attached to the house, an outdoor room creates a smooth transition between inside and outdoors. Outdoor rooms can range from a sun room to a spot in the garden that is screened or sheltered (by trellis, an awning, or some other method). Arbors, pergolas, gazebos, pavilions, summerhouses, porches, conservatories, and balconies all offer ways to enjoy nature in relative comfort.

**RIGHT:** Cane furniture is a traditional choice for conservatories and other "outdoor rooms." This pared-down wooden structure offers shelter from the elements while showcasing the rural idyll outside.

**RIGHT:** Here, the owners have brought the outside in using an array of plants and flowers to complement the view. Comfortable seating encourages the visitor to linger among the foliage.

# VIEW FINDER

The whole point of a sun room is the wall of windows overlooking the garden or view of the landscape, so here's how to make the most of this vista:

- **Windows serve to frame the view. Seeing less of something can actually give it more emphasis.**
- **If the glazed area is large enough, what is just outside will appear to be part of the sun room, so plan its arrangement carefully, whether it is furniture, flowers, trees, the framework of a pergola, or a balustrade.**
- **Spotlighting these features at night can make the window seem to disappear, extending the sun room into the enchanting scene outside.**

**RIGHT:** With its wall-to-wall French doors and windows above them, this sun room is not only gloriously sunny, but it can also have nearly all of one side opened up to the garden, so that indoors and out merge.

**MAXIMUM EXPOSURE:**
The weathered look is by
definition the perfect
finish for furniture in an
outdoor room.

**TOP FAR LEFT:** White painted
chairs and benches work
with elegant white walls to
create a space that is light
and airy. Plump cushions
make this a place to linger.

**TOP LEFT:** Old wood-slatted
garden chairs with their
faded, peeling paintwork
look totally at home here,
but if you don't already have
a suitably weather-beaten
set, it's not cheating to
buy the chairs at flea
markets or even to distress
some brand-new ones.

**BOTTOM FAR LEFT:** A painted
Lloyd Loom-style chair is
a classic choice indoors
or out. Look out for vintage
outdoor furniture in thrift
stores or flea markets,
or alternatively choose
inexpensive versions
available from many stores.

**BOTTOM LEFT:** Tie-on
cushions make simple
metal folding chairs more
comfortable and create
an uncluttered look in this
orangery that really does blur
the boundaries between the
house and garden.

Both the function and the structure of the outdoor
room obviously determine what furnishings are used.
An enclosed porch, conservatory, or sun room, which
offers full, year-round protection from the weather,
could therefore be furnished with anything suitable for
the rest of the house. However, furniture with an
outdoor feel to it—such as wicker, cane, rattan, twig,
painted wood with a distressed finish, rustic wood, cast
iron, or cast aluminum—usually looks best, particularly
if made comfortable with squashy cushions. Avoid
anything too fussy, and aim for a relaxed informality.

In a gazebo, open porch, or other outdoor room with
just a roof, outdoor furniture that is not totally
weatherproof could be used, so long as it is portable
enough to bring indoors during spells of bad weather
and at the end of the season. However, cotton or linen
covers will be prone to fading and mildew, so it might
be preferable to choose outdoor furniture covered with
one of the new super-synthetics that resemble natural
fibers but are much more weather-resistant.

**BELOW:** In this unconven-
tional room different furniture
styles coexist quite happily.
This is an eclectic mix where
anything goes.

On a narrow balcony or patio, or in an arbor or other outdoor room that offers little protection against sun and rain, only fully weatherproof furniture like teak Adirondack chairs and picnic tables should be left in place for any length of time. However, this can be supplemented with portable pieces that are put away at night, and when combined with table linens, pillows, blankets, and vases of flowers, it can look completely magical.

Lighting plays a big part in creating atmosphere in an outdoor room used at night. For outdoor rooms in the garden, use electric lanterns, spotlights trained on foliage, or uplights concealed among shrubs to provide dramatic lighting that isn't too bright.

**ABOVE:** Potted plants look nice in any outdoor room. Place them on wire plant stands, wall brackets, windowsills—even the table, where they make a charming centerpiece.

## LIGHT AND SHADE

For a successful outdoor room you must be able to control whether the sun streams in or not. Try these ideas:

- **Shutters, blinds, or shades at windows can be shut at will in a sun room or conservatory.**
- **At the sunny end of a porch, fit blinds within a wood frame. Or insert jumbo grommets into the top and bottom of some canvas and slot onto horizontal rods at floor and ceiling level.**
- **An electrically controlled retractable awning can be installed to produce shade at the push of a button.**

**BELOW:** An outdoor room is a delightful place for summer meals. To seat a large number of people, a wallpapering table can be given an elegance and panache fit for a banquet.

If you don't have exterior lighting you could use solar lights on walls or spikes in the ground. Candles in hurricane lamps or pierced lanterns are essential for tables, while votives in glass jars can be hung from wires and dotted all around the outdoor room, to create dancing points of light. In a conservatory, prevent harsh reflections in the glass by using a lot of low-wattage light sources instead of just a few bright ones. An old chandelier would complete the magical atmosphere.

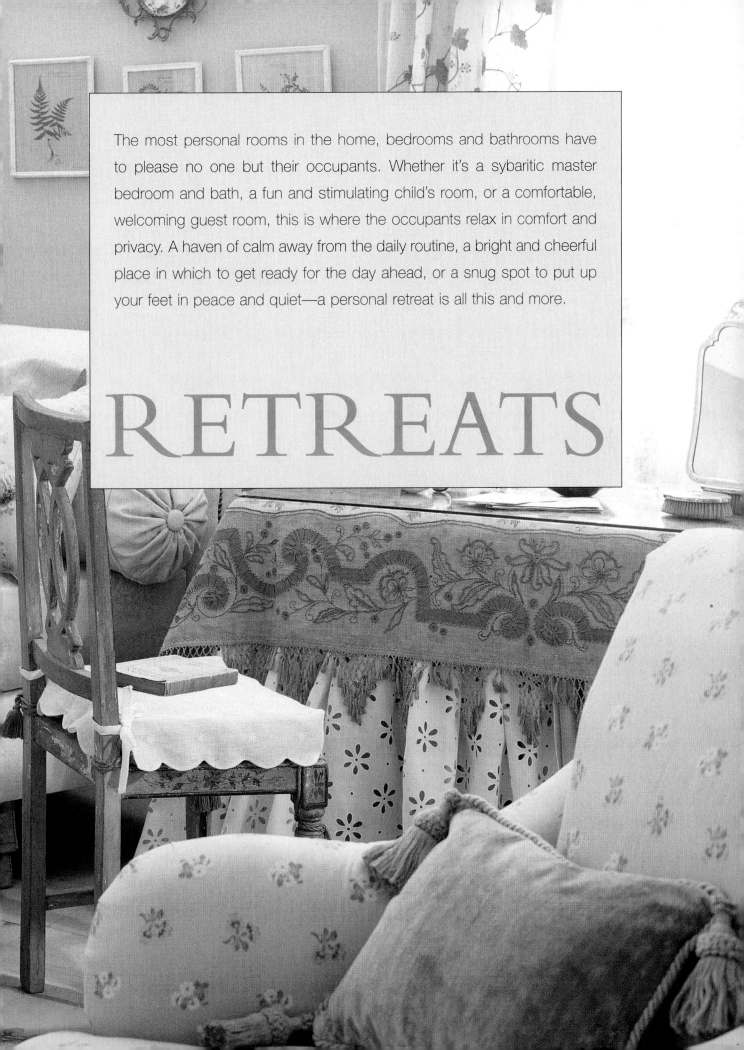

The most personal rooms in the home, bedrooms and bathrooms have to please no one but their occupants. Whether it's a sybaritic master bedroom and bath, a fun and stimulating child's room, or a comfortable, welcoming guest room, this is where the occupants relax in comfort and privacy. A haven of calm away from the daily routine, a bright and cheerful place in which to get ready for the day ahead, or a snug spot to put up your feet in peace and quiet—a personal retreat is all this and more.

# RETREATS

# BEDROOMS

A bedroom can be as simple or as indulgent as you wish, but whatever your tastes, remember that although bedrooms are used for everything from watching television to riding a stationary bike, the primary purpose of the room is relaxation. Whatever you choose to put in your bedroom it is imperative that you get a good night's sleep, so the basic requirement is a comfortable bed. Having said that, the bedroom is the ideal place to make your decorating dreams come true, whether you crave calm minimalism or the opulence of a palace fit for a queen. The right colors, fabrics, lighting, and furnishings can make your bedroom a great place to be.

**RIGHT:** The ultimate in romance, this opulent boudoir conjures up eighteenth-century elegance and provides a complete haven from the stresses of modern life.

# BEDROOM COLORS

Subdued colors usually work best in the bedroom. Bedrooms should be the most restful rooms in the home, and soft, gentle colors are the most tranquil. They relax you at night when you go to bed, and they cheer you up first thing in the morning.

Accents in strong colors will prevent the room from looking bland. These are the invigorating hues, which energize you and enliven your decorating scheme, so use them for a chair, curtains, a bedspread, flowers, pillows, rugs, or perhaps a whole wall. Add definition with a few dark tones, in an iron curtain rod or in a dark wood floor, mirror frame, four-poster bedstead, or chest of drawers. (Too much dark wood, however, could seem oppressive.)

Gentle colors create a feminine effect, so if you want a more masculine-looking room, use patterns like plaids, along with deeper accent shades and a palette based on strong neutrals such as putty gray with mustard, cream, and eggplant. There is definitely a place for neutrals in any bedroom, masculine or feminine. An all-white or white and cream decor works well here, as you can include crisp white sheets, vintage textiles, and plenty of lace, for a serenely romantic boudoir.

Colors that are near each other on the color wheel (see page 25), such as apricot and primrose yellow, or sky blue and apple green, will look the most harmonious together, and they can be sharpened up with the crisp contrast of white woodwork, accessories, or painted furniture.

For a livelier effect, use a palette of softened contrasts (see page 29), incorporating tones of colors that are roughly opposite each other on the color wheel, like lilac and primrose yellow, or old rose and moss green.

**LEFT:** A range of contrasting colors adds interest to a romantic white and sand scheme. White bed linen looks great for a fresh effect and a traditional look, while the white-painted bedstead blends into the background, creating a calm, spacious atmosphere.

**RIGHT:** In this bedroom the dark wood of the bedstead, picture frames, and chair provides a pleasing amount of tonal contrast. The blue of the bedcover looks lovely with dark wood.

In a small room, limiting the decor to two colors will make it seem more spacious. Even in a larger room, a two-color scheme is more calming than one containing three colors because there is less color contrast. To compensate for the limited number of colors, add a greater degree of textural contrast.

If soft tones are too quiet for you, even with a liberal use of accents, then don't worry about trying to make the scheme restful—just choose colors you like to have around you. This is, after all, your own private place. If you have very little wall space, perhaps because of large windows and closets, the walls could be painted or papered in quite a strong color without becoming overpowering. Add white bed hangings and woodwork for a crisp, fresh look.

As always, make your starting point something that contains the colors you want to use, such as a favorite quilt or a patterned fabric, rug, or wallpaper. If you don't want to use wallpaper over the entire wall area, you could create panels with narrow molding and then wallpaper inside the panels.

**LEFT:** A harmonious blend of orange tints creates a warm and peaceful atmosphere in this bedroom. When two tones are used on a wall above and below a chair rail, the darker tone generally looks best on the lower portion; a darker tone on the upper portion would create a top-heavy effect.

# GOOD ACCENTS

Add visual punch to a soft color palette with contrasting accent colors:

- **Apricot with blue, soft blue-green, green, yellow, or terra-cotta**
- **Buttercup yellow with dark red, dark blue, lavender, or brown**
- **Pale primrose yellow with reddish purple or gray-blue**
- **Pale lime green with bright turquoise or terra-cotta**
- **Apple green with pink or terra-cotta**
- **Gray-green with orange, peacock blue, or crimson**
- **Light blue-green with pale rose, rust, or burgundy**
- **Gray-blue with raspberry or coral**
- **Cornflower blue with yellow, orange, red, or green**
- **Soft gray-violet with green or burnt orange**
- **Amethyst with turquoise or leaf green**
- **Plaster pink with blue-green or gray-green**

**ABOVE:** The classic combination of red, white, blue, and green looks crisp and fresh on checks and stripes. Displaying bed linen and blankets offers a relatively inexpensive way of creating or reinforcing a color scheme.

**RIGHT:** A patchwork quilt provides an excellent starting point for the decor. If you are making the quilt to go with the room, you can use fabrics that will appear elsewhere, in the bed skirt, window treatment, or pillow shams.

**LEFT:** An antique giltwood bed with a canework head and foot, a luxurious quilt, and sumptuous pillows makes this bedroom exude sheer glamour.

**ABOVE:** An open doorway affords a tantalizing glimpse of this elegant bedroom. The sleek ottoman and sparkling chandelier give it the feel of a sophisticated sitting room.

# CREATING AN ATMOSPHERE

Bedrooms offer an excellent opportunity to create a special atmosphere. However, keep in mind whatever roles the room has to fulfill—wall-to-wall luxury may seem rather incongruous if you are also using the room as an exercise center or home office.

Every major element—colors, textures, patterns, lighting, furniture, wall and floor coverings, window treatments, and, most of all, the bed—will contribute to the atmosphere, as will more ephemeral aspects like scented candles and flowers. For example, if you like floral motifs, you could create a flowery bower with sprigged wallpaper, floral fabrics, simple country furniture, whitewashed floorboards, and such colors as cream with splashes of clover, lilac, cornflower, buttercup, terra-cotta, and leaf. Or go for a French provincial style, with white walls, a terra-cotta floor or natural matting, heavy lace curtains, and bright-colored Provençal print fabrics. The English country-house look is another floral option, with splashy chintzes, well-worn Oriental rugs, and antique furniture.

## SHEER ROMANCE

Floaty white fabrics and lace are essential for a romantic boudoir:

- **Use diaphanous muslin, dotted swiss, printed voile, sheer linen, or panels of lace at the windows and as bed hangings.**
- **Swathe dressing tables and quilt racks in more of the same.**
- **Make short tablecloths for nightstands from lace or eyelet (broderie anglaise).**
- **Trim the lower edge of the bed skirt with lace—or make a skirt from one of these feminine fabrics.**

151

ABOVE: Curtains, pillow shams, towels, and even a nightshirt contribute to the overall impression of just-laundered freshness in this bedroom.

# TEXTILES

Textiles can have an enormous impact on bedrooms—indeed, it's possible to create a whole new look using nothing but fabric. Whether you prefer the airy lightness of muslin, lawn, and voile; the simplicity and naturalness of cotton, gingham, and linen; the tactile textures of wool, jumbo corduroy, velvet, suede, and chenille; or the opulence of silk taffeta and brocade, there are bound to be fabrics to suit your own style.

Even in a minimalistic bedroom, there is a place for textiles, from the fitted bedcover to the sleek shades at the windows. And in an unabashedly feminine room, a generous use of fabric produces a delightful feeling of comfort and self-indulgence. The principal uses of fabric are at the windows and on the bed. Bed hangings and window treatments are no longer expected to match, but they should be visually linked. Other opportunities for using textiles in the bedroom include a dressing table

RIGHT: Crisp black and white stripes prevent a cloying effect on this dressing table skirt and coordinating cover for the chair seat. A sheer canopy softens the hard edge of the black mirror.

RIGHT: A stack of neatly folded quilts in similar patterns and coordinating colors shows how different fabrics can maintain a visual link.

BELOW RIGHT: This flouncy footstool cover brings a splash of bright color, while the small surface area keeps the effect on the room subtle.

skirt, a fabric screen, small tablecloths for nightstands, plus cushions, slipcovers, and upholstery for seating.

Prevent small bedrooms from seeming to be awash in fabric by choosing solid-color or subtly patterned textiles in light tones. Or, if you are using a patterned fabric or wallpaper, combine it with unpatterned textiles, or a stripe or check in the same colors.

Fabric on the walls can create a lavish effect. If the same is used at the windows, you will create a cozy, "cocooning" effect. With "upholstered" walls, or "walling," fabric is stretched over a padded framework of battens or panels, and the edges are trimmed with decorative braid. Another approach is to hang fabric curtains from continuous rods all around the walls, tying them back at doors, windows, fireplaces, etc. For an even more sumptuous, "tented" effect, walls and/or the ceiling can be draped in fabric. With either technique, inexpensive materials such as muslin, lining fabric, extra-wide sheeting, or sari fabric can be used.

## ALL IN THE DETAIL

Clever detailing can transform a plain fabric into something with real impact. Consider some of these ideas when you plan your soft furnishings:

- **Piping in a contrasting solid color**
- **A line of buttons, whether antique bone, mother-of-pearl, wood, bright-colored, or fabric-covered**
- **Ties in a coordinating material**
- **Narrow binding in a small stripe or check**
- **Parallel lines of ribbon**
- **Rickrack (zigzag-shaped braid) edging**
- **A contrasting band of fabric along the edge**

# BEDROOM WINDOWS

You can be as bold as you like with the window treatments in a bedroom, so long as they are also functional, providing privacy, filtering sun, and blocking light as required. Layering is one way of satisfying both aesthetic and practical requirements, because you can use blinds or shades next to the window and curtains on top. (See pages 46–9 for advice on layering and on curtains in general.)

Remember that intricate styles can detract from an atmosphere of tranquility, so it's safer to err on the side of simplicity, but this does not mean that you have to opt for minimalism. Today's window fashions feature beautiful textures and informal styles, often with striking top treatments (similar to those sometimes used for bed hangings—see page 162). In addition, there are the ever-popular rod-pocket curtains slotted over tension wires or rods, and the classic pinch pleats, goblet pleats, and other types of shirred or pleated headings made by hand or using self-styling tapes (see page 47).

For a refreshingly simple alternative to pleated curtains, hang café curtains or even lightweight full-length curtains from a thin pole using clip-on rings, which consist of clips that attach to the fabric, and rings for the pole to slot through. For extra

**ABOVE:** Sheer curtains tied to a rod above the window echo the bed curtains in this bedroom. The dainty integral valance on the window curtains is made by stitching a band with a zigzag-shaped edge to the top of the curtains and folding it over to the front.

**LEFT:** Translucent lace panels are attached to the wall above a pair of windows for a pretty but unfussy treatment that provides privacy and lets light flood in while keeping bright sunlight at bay.

**WORKING IN PAIRS**

In attics, the best window treatment is one that is unified and also uses the same colors as for the walls. Here, matching tailored valances with corner pleats are used above a pair of windows, and only an outer curtain is used at each window.

interest, fold over several inches at the top prior to attaching the clips to create an integral valance. These clips are only strong enough for use with a lightweight fabric.

For a simple look, flat lengths of fabric such as lace panels can be simply attached to the wall above a window with special fixings, or mounted onto a multi-track gliding panel system. Weighted at the bottom, the fabric panels slide horizontally along separate tracks within the casing. The system allows you to combine translucent and opaque panels, adjusting their positions as required.

Roman shades are an increasingly popular window treatment. When extended to cover the window, they are flat, and they are pulled up into horizontal folds. The folds are either floppy or stiffened with hidden slats so that they are straight and crisp.

When choosing fabrics, think also about trimmings. For example, rich damask curtains could be edged with crystal beads, or a white organdy Roman shade trimmed with leather. Even something as simple as jumbo rickrack (zigzag-shaped braid) or grosgrain ribbon can look fantastic on the right fabric, such as a ticking. Contrasting fabric can be used as trimming, too—try a scalloped or zigzag-shaped band decorating the leading edge of a curtain or lower edge of a shade.

# BED IDEAS

The bed is the dominant feature of a bedroom, so it's important to make it worthy of attention. Vintage beds are among the most highly sought after of all antiques, and indeed there are some beautiful examples to choose from. One of the most graceful is the sleigh bed, named for its lovely scrolled ends. Usually in a handsome wood, it makes an elegant daybed, particularly with a bolster at each end and a fitted cover. Vintage brass and painted iron bedsteads also look beautifully romantic. A wide variety of old wooden bedsteads is available, some of them with canework head and footboards, and these look attractive whether natural, stained, or painted. The most popular style of all is the four-poster, or full tester, because of the canopy (or "tester") extending the full length of the bed and supported by the posts. Some canopies were flat, others curved or serpentine-shaped, and curtains were traditionally hung from them. Half testers have shorter, flat canopies, again traditionally with curtains. Some beds have the four-poster frame but no wooden canopy at the top.

Antique beds are not always in good condition or large enough, and you may have difficulty in getting a modern mattress to fit. As a result, there is a healthy market in

**RIGHT:** A fabric cover tied over the end of the open wooden footboard makes this bed more enclosed and cozy.

**BELOW RIGHT:** Fabric draped over a metal framework affixed to the ceiling and one wall creates a contemporary version of the four-poster in this sophisticated bedroom.

**BELOW:** Narrow curtains hung from rods affixed at right angles to the wall at ceiling height on either side of a bed resemble the hangings on a traditional half tester.

reproduction beds, which combine the styling of bygone days with all the advantages of a modern bed. And even if you don't have a complete bedstead, you can create the look of one with a headboard, and perhaps posts attached to the corners of a modern base. Also, hangings can be used to simulate a four-poster effect (see page 162).

Imaginative textile treatments or other strategies can transform plainer beds into beautiful objects in their own right (see pages 158–63). Whatever the style, don't be hidebound about the bed's position. The traditional position is with the head against the wall, or sometimes, if the bed is a twin, sideways against the wall. However, placing it across a corner, or even "floating" like an island in the center of the room, can sometimes be more effective, both visually and in the use of space. Or it could go under the window, with the curtains serving as a theatrical backdrop.

**ABOVE:** A central inverted pleat with a neatly buttoned placket is the focal point of this beautifully simple bed skirt, creating an elegant base for the rest of the bed treatment.

# BED SKIRTS

Even though it is scarcely more than a foot high, a skirt is a crucial element in a bed treatment, not only covering up whatever is under the bed but also creating a neat finish for the bedcover. A bed skirt consists of four sides sewn to a top, which sits between the base and the mattress (the top can therefore be made from a cheap fabric such as sheeting). There has to be some fullness to allow for people accidentally kicking it, so either inverted pleats are used at the corners and sometimes in the center, or the fullness is distributed evenly all around in gathers or box pleats, depending on the effect you prefer.

The style, fabric, and trimmings should be in keeping with the rest of the bed treatment, but bed skirts can be so beautiful that you might even want to make the bedcover subordinate to the skirt. The bedcover should overlap the top edge of the skirt, but the amount of skirt that is left showing will depend on the desired effect. Even a very narrow strip of visible fabric can have a big impact.

If the bed has attractive legs you may not wish to use a skirt at all. Why not upholster the bed base with a fabric such as gingham or ticking, and tuck the bedcover in under the mattress, for a clean, tailored, and very chic look?

**RIGHT:** Embroidered sheer fabric forms soft gathers in this romantic skirt, its fragility matching the delicacy of the metal bedstead. To stop a skirt looking fussy, just allow less of it to show.

## SWEET AND LOW

Try one of these snazzy skirts:

- **Ticking skirt with an eyelet (broderie anglaise) "petticoat" just showing underneath**
- **Skirt made from vintage lace sheets with a shaped edge**
- **Sleek natural linen skirt matching a tailored linen bedcover, with parallel lines of black overlock stitching along lower edge**
- **Gingham skirt with crochet lace trim**

# BEDCLOTHES & PILLOWS

Because the bed is the largest, most noticeable feature of the room, and because the made-up bed is viewed from above, the bedclothes and any pillows on the bed are what stand out most. On a king-size bed, this area is massive—which is why it's important to take some care over what you put on the bed. It is also the reason that a change of bedcover can dramatically alter the look of a room.

The bedcover you choose should reflect not only your decor but also the style of the bed, though for any given bed, there is, of course, a whole range of possibilities that would look good. A heavy wooden bedstead, for example, would look great with an Amish-style quilt, as the large, richly colored sections of the geometric pattern would counterbalance the mass of the bed—but it could equally be covered in masses of crisp white lace and eyelet (broderie anglaise), to contrast with the dark wood. A modern bed could look sleek and chic with a graphic-patterned duvet, or rich and opulent with a wide-striped taffeta headboard and a fringed bedspread of richly colored vintage brocade. Dress a white-painted brass or iron bed with a romantic patchwork quilt with piles of pillows on top, or a sharp-looking comforter in a strong solid color with decorative quilting, topped by plaid moiré pillows.

Old textiles can be used to create wonderful effects. Use small lace items, from collars to placemats, to make up or decorate pillow shams. Cut pieces from worn-out patchwork quilts to make covers for toss pillows. An antique kilim, an old plaid blanket, or a Navajo rug could look wonderful as a bedcover. Modern textiles, too, can create a particular feeling. For sheer opulence, add piles of pillows made from felted wool, cashmere, pashmina, fleece, mohair, fake fur, or tapestry fabric. A throw or folded textile at the end of the bed adds contrasting color and texture, whether it is a blanket, a paisley shawl, or a fake zebra-skin print. (For more about pillows and throws, see pages 74–7.)

**BELOW:** Pretty trimmings and dainty tucks add textural interest to this inviting treatment in peaches and cream.

**FAR LEFT:** Toss pillows, a pillow sham, and a flouncy bolster in an assortment of patterns and solids but a limited color range look cheerful and upbeat against a gingham headboard.

**TOP LEFT:** Gingham comes in all scales, and a tiny check is ideal for making dainty bows on this crisp-looking pillow sham.

**BOTTOM LEFT:** This strictly controlled red and white scheme makes a strong classical statement.

# BED HANGINGS

Although the original purpose of bed hangings—to keep out drafts and prevent creepie-crawlies in the roof from falling into the bed—is no longer a priority, they do give a bed an undeniable stature, while also softening the overall impression. The traditional treatment of a four-poster (full-tester) bed includes a fabric canopy over the top, a valance beneath that, and lined curtains that can be fully closed at each corner. However, you could just have narrow, unlined curtains that stay permanently open at the corners—or no curtains or valance but just a canopy over the top, hanging down about 8–10 inches. This can look gorgeous in a fine handkerchief linen or simple homespun check. (Another option is to leave the framework completely unadorned, which can suit a contemporary-style home, particularly if the posts are delicately tapered.) If you don't have a four-poster, you can create a similar

curtained effect by affixing curtain rods to the ceiling, following the shape of the bed. Using a double-rod set will allow you to have a valance as well as curtains.

The method of attaching curtains to the framework of a four-poster can be decorative in itself. Many of the techniques are the same as for attaching window curtains to a pole. Jumbo grommets, for example, can be inserted into the top of a curtain and then simply slotted onto the rod or pole. Or the curtain can be tied on using lengths of ribbon or cord through the grommets, or using fabric ties stitched into the top edge of the curtain. For a more tailored look, you can use looped fabric tabs, which are stitched into the curtain top so that the pole or rod can be slotted through them.

A half tester bed has a shortened canopy and lined curtains around the head of the bed only. To create a similar effect on a twin bed, affix a half-round corona—in effect, a semicircular shelf—to the wall or ceiling above the head of the bed, and hang curtains from that. Or simply gather the curtains onto a curtain rod that has a short return at each end, projecting at right angles, and mount this on the wall. For a twin bedstead placed sideways against the wall, the fabric wraps right around the headboard and footboard, where it is tied back to create a cozy, tented effect.

A dramatic way of draping a bed with hangings when it has no framework of its own is to suspend curtain poles from the ceiling, just above the head and foot of the bed. Drape a long length of fabric (the same width as the bed) over them, so that it reaches to the floor at each end. (It will have to be attached to the poles with staples or hook-and-loop tape.)

A wide variety of fabrics are suitable for bed hangings, ranging from antique linen to crewelwork fabric or silk. But because a lot of yardage is required, inexpensive material like muslin, sheeting, and curtain lining is often used and can look just as romantic and lavish as costlier textiles.

**ABOVE:** Producing a dreamy, languorous look that would be at home in the deep South, these curtains are simply tied to the metal frame of the bed.

**FAR LEFT:** Each of these translucent curtains is attached to the metal frame by means of a narrow casing stitched halfway along the length, through which the removable rod is slotted.

**LEFT:** Yet another way to create hangings on a bed framework is simply to sling lengths of fabric over the top. In reality, though, hook-and-loop tape or staples hidden on top of the frame are necessary to keep them in place.

# HEADBOARD IDEAS

A headboard gives a modern bed definition and importance, making it look more like a bedstead. Upholstered headboards are deservedly popular because they provide something comfortable to lean against while reading in bed, keeping your head away from the wall. If you don't like your existing upholstered headboard, it is probably a simple matter to cover it with a chic new fabric or a slipcover that can be removed for laundering. For a sharper look, try a headboard in wood, cane, wicker, chrome, brass, painted iron, or plexiglas. Bear in mind how heavy it will look relative to your other furnishings—an openwork metal headboard, for example, will look lighter than a carved wooden one. Think about how it will look with the bedcover, pillows, and bed skirt, too. A very large, plain headboard covered in the same fabric as that used for the bed skirt would make a graphic background for, say, a simple duvet in a contrasting color.

To create a headboard effect, place a folding screen, a large old iron or wooden gate, or a trellis with posts between the wall and the bed. Or build a half-height room-divider away from the wall, with shelves for cupboards on one side and the bed on the

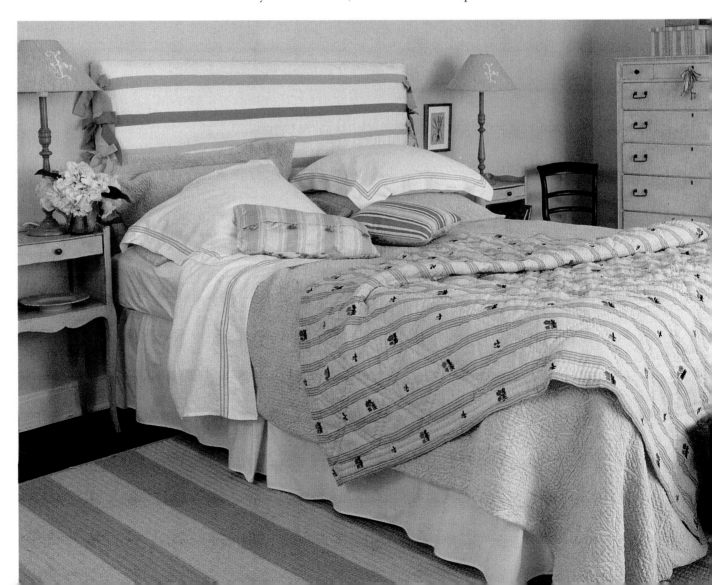

other. For comfort, you could hang flat box pillows (using fabric ties or loops stitched into the seams) from a narrow curtain pole or dowel affixed to the divider. Match the fabric or some piping to one of the fabrics used on the bed.

Using something that makes a strong visual statement on the wall above the headboard will give the bed greater impact. This could be anything from a single, oversize poster or black and white photograph, to a huge monogram, or several large squares of solid color painted straight onto the wall. A single curtain could look good—affix a curtain pole to the wall near the ceiling, and either slot this through a casing in the fabric or attach the curtain using a self-styling tape (see page 47) that forms a decorative heading, such as smocking. Another idea is to hang a flat panel of lace or other attractive textile on the wall by bunching it around a line of curtain bosses at the top.

**LEFT:** A plain headboard has been embellished with ribbon stitched along the length and tied at the ends.

**TOP:** A simple monogram on an elegantly shaped linen-covered headboard makes a subtle personal statement.

**ABOVE:** This salvaged piece of architectural wrought-iron gives the impression of a much grander bed.

# DISGUISING BEDS

In a one-room apartment or in a bedroom that doubles as a sitting room or home office, it is likely that the bed will need to be disguised in some way. The simplest method is to make it look like somewhere to sit, but this will really only work for a twin bed, placed sideways against the wall. If there are two twin beds in a room, they could be placed against adjacent walls, with a square table between them in the corner where they meet. Pillows need to be hidden away, or at least tucked into attractive pillow shams, and toss pillows added. A fitted, tailored, floor-length bedcover will look more appropriate than a frilly, feminine one with a bed skirt.

Another approach for a twin bed placed sideways against the wall is to dress it up as a daybed. It should be given a fitted cover, as above, and a bolster placed at each end; the length of the bolster should correspond to the width of the bed. A pole one foot long is mounted on the wall so it projects outward, then a single length of fabric is draped over it, held in place by a narrow casing that slots onto the pole. The fabric drapes gracefully over the ends of the bed, creating an elegant Empire-style daybed.

**CALL IT A DAYBED**
If a bedstead is attractive enough, a fitted cover for the mattress can be used instead of a bedcover, as here in a ticking cover that is piped around the edges. With the addition of simple hangings, all color-coordinated, a bedstead is transformed into a chic daybed.

**LEFT:** This bed in an alcove has been dressed up with pillows and a throw to make a window seat. The curtain can be closed to create privacy for the sleeper.

Instead of hanging fabric from a pole above a twin bed, you could tuck the bed into an alcove or into a space between built-in closets, with curtains at the front. If you have a twin bedstead with decorative ends, such as a sleigh bed, this will need very little in the way of disguise, because it already looks like a daybed.

Double beds are too wide to disguise, but they can be hidden (as can twin beds). One way of doing this is to put the bed high up on a platform or mezzanine, with your living space beneath. A fold-down, Murphy-type bed is also a good way of getting the bed out of sight.

Choosing alternative designs is another way of hiding the bed. A sofa bed is one of the most obvious examples, as the sofa can be pulled out and transformed into a bed (twin or double, depending on the length of the sofa). There are many styles to choose from, including chair beds, daybeds, and futon sofas. In addition, plain, one-person futons provide seating by day when folded up and placed on a seating frame, and a convenient sleeping surface by night when unfolded. A trundle bed is a possibility, too, as it is stored underneath a conventional single bed. In some designs, a twin bed can be converted into a double bed by pulling out a smaller bed from underneath and unfolding the legs to make it the same height as the main bed, so that the two can be made up as one double bed.

**LEFT:** Piling the daybed with pillows and bolsters provides the ideal opportunity to introduce beautiful fabrics to your room, without breaking the bank.

**RIGHT:** This attractive wrought iron daybed placed under the window creates an irresistible focal point. The view through the window, the flowers and accessories on the windowsill, and the luxurious pillows all help to disguise the fact that this is a bed.

# BEDROOM STORAGE

Bedrooms never seem to be big enough. There is always more clothing, accessories, and other items than there is storage space. By the time the bed is accommodated, the storage pieces have to be fitted into whatever odd spaces are left over. Yet a lack of clutter and an overall tidiness are essential if the bedroom is to be a calm haven.

The first step is to pare down what needs to be stored, moving your possessions to more appropriate rooms (or the attic) or discarding them if you haven't worn them or used them recently. Once you have reduced your belongings to the things you actually need to have near you, decide what your storage needs are and consider how your bedroom can be adapted to cater for them. Are most of your clothes separates, which can be hung in two tiers in the closet, or do you have a lot of long dresses, which need full-length hanging space? Are most of your clothes jeans and sweaters that can be stored folded on shelves or in drawers? Do you have umpteen pairs of expensive shoes that you would like to store in cubbyholes that will protect them from damage? Will you want to house an expanding collection of books in the bedroom? Fundamental questions like these have to be answered before you can proceed.

Built-in storage provides the most efficient use of space. It can take a number of forms. For example, you could have closets either side of an alcove for a bed fitted into it lengthwise (see page 168), or a low platform bed with cupboards or drawers underneath. Though associated with children's rooms, these can look very stylish and grown-up if well designed, and they don't have to be particularly high. You could even combine these two ideas, building a platform bed in an alcove between

**RIGHT:** Bedroom storage is about more than clothes. Don't forget to allow sufficient storage for bulky bed linen, such as these traditional quilts.

**BELOW:** Using chests of drawers beside the bed instead of nightstands provides extra storage space as well as a larger surface for lamps, books, and other bedtime necessities.

## LATERAL THINKING

It's amazing what you can annex as storage space when you put your mind to it. Here are some possibilities:

- **Fit alcoves with hanging rails or shelves, and conceal them with curtains.**
- **Put a round piece of plywood on top of a small file cabinet (securing it with removable heavy-duty double-sided tape) and cover with a pretty tablecloth.**
- **Use the space under a dressing table or other table with a skirt for storing anything from exercise equipment to an electric hairdryer.**
- **If your bed doesn't have built-in drawers, keep shallow plastic or wicker boxes under the bed to hold bed linen, blankets, and tablecloths.**

closets, with drawers beneath and bookshelves inside the alcove. A conventional bed with its head against the wall could also be backed by shelves.

Built-in storage has to be planned carefully so that the architectural character and proportions of the room are not spoiled. If the closets or cabinets will cover one of the longer walls, make sure that the room will not seem too narrow as a result. If they will be tucked into alcoves, decide whether the effect will be too uniform and uninteresting. Blend the built-in cabinets into the room by including baseboards and coves that match those in the rest of the room, and match materials and colors where appropriate. To prevent built-in cabinets from looking too dull or austere, avoid having a line of solid doors. Break up the expanse with color, shelves and drawers, matchboarding, glass doors, interesting details such as moldings and nice handles (perhaps

RIGHT: Capacious old blanket boxes, chests, and trunks are invaluable for storing bulky things like bedding. When its top is clear, this blanket box can double as a window seat. If there is room, pieces like this also look good at the end of the bed.

LEFT: Vintage case furniture such as this painted cupboard often seems more at home in a country-style decor than sleek built-in storage.

leather, brushed steel, faceted glass, or colored resin), or a variety of different materials. You could cleverly camouflage closets by fitting flush doors with magnetic catches, which you then either paint or cover with wallpaper or fabric to match your walls. (Do not add handles or you would defeat the object of the exercise.)

If you already have built-in cabinets, changing the handles is a quick and easy way to jazz them up, and it works with closets, too. On paneled doors, the panels could be replaced with trellis, cane, brass mesh, punched tin, or fabric (see page 96). On some closet doors it may be easier to cover the panels with fabric than to remove them.

Although it takes more space, freestanding furniture does offer greater flexibility. Tall pieces, such as an armoire or highboy, not only offer extra storage for

the same floor space as low pieces, but also have an aesthetic value, providing important vertical lines and balancing the mass of the bed. Too many of these would look oppressive and cramped, so you'll also want low pieces such as a chest of drawers. Remember that freestanding pieces need space around them to show them off to best effect.

### STACKS OF SPACE
Every little bit helps when it comes to storage, so use your imagination to collect small items that will add up to a fair bit of extra storage. Stacks of wooden, leather, metal, or canvas boxes, old leather suitcases, and lidded wicker baskets look great, add texture, and can store a multitude of things, from jewelry to sewing paraphernalia.

**RIGHT:** Modern white cabinets with simple lines keep this bedroom free of clutter, creating a restful haven. Even the most dedicated follower of fashion will find a place for everything here.

# OCCASIONAL FURNITURE

Occasional furniture allows you to reconcile all the various uses of your bedroom. With appropriate pieces, the bedroom can double as a sitting room or den, to use throughout the day as well as at night. Because it is a non-public space, it tends to attract all those funny old pieces that are too small or too rustic, or just don't fit in anywhere else—which is part of its charm but also can be the room's decorative undoing. That beloved old rocking chair your grandmother passed down to you can happily sit here next to the writing desk that didn't look good enough for the living room, but try not to wind up with a jumble of incompatible pieces that have no visual coherence. A spacious bedroom is actually more at risk of this happening than a small room, because it will act like a magnet for pieces that are not only unrelated but also too small. In fact, it could be argued that the bedroom is where you should put your finest, most delicate pieces of furniture, because they are away from the rough and tumble of family life and parties. In a small bedroom, light, open-back chairs and glass tables seem to take up less space because the eye looks through them as if they weren't there.

**LEFT:** Use slipcovers to bring visual coherence to mismatched chairs that have found their way into your bedroom. The fabrics don't have to match, provided that the patterns, if any, look fine together (see pages 34–5), but the colors should relate to other items in the room to provide a visual link. Similarly, disparate pieces of wood furniture may need nothing more than a coat of paint to tie them together.

# WHITE AND LIGHT

A light and airy approach is especially well suited to bedrooms, so try some of these ideas:

- **Use floaty, diaphanous sheers not just on windows but also on screens and as bed hangings.**
- **Paint wood or iron furniture in white or a light color.**
- **Make slipcovers for chairs in these same pale tones.**
- **Collect vintage linen textiles to use as soft furnishings throughout the bedroom.**

**ABOVE:** Even the coat hanger has been carefully selected for its aesthetic qualities in this ethereal still life. Based around a simple screen, it captures the highly sought-after atmosphere of romance and femininity.

**RIGHT:** In interior decoration, it's often the thoughtful little touches that make the big difference. What may seem the least functional pieces of furniture can set the overall tone more than anything else, as with this simple white bedroom table.

**BEDSIDE MANNERS**

Furniture placed at the foot of a bed can add a certain grandeur, and provides a separate furniture zone within the room. Although a chest or settee is more usual, a writing table accompanied by an occasional chair is the perfect addition to the multifunctional bedroom and is large enough not to be dwarfed by the bed. Drawers offer handy storage for stationery, and a pair of candle lamps provide atmospheric illumination.

Apart from the dressing table (see page 181), the most essential items of occasional furniture are nightstands. If you don't use chests of drawers next to the bed (see page 170), you'll need bedside tables or cabinets that are big enough to be functional. A matching pair isn't necessary, so long as they are the same height (which must be at least as high as the top of the mattress).

If you can possibly incorporate a sitting area, do so. All you need is a comfortable easy chair, a lamp, and a little table, but a second chair—or a love seat—makes it not just a solitary reading area but also a sociable place for a chat. Tuck it into a corner or by a window or bookcase. If there is room for the table to serve as a writing desk or hobby table, you will extend the versatility of the room still further.

Alternatively, you might be able to place them at the end of the bed. This can look very effective, grounding the bed in much the same way that a headboard does. However, the piece must be substantial enough not to look silly next to the bed. A chaise longue, love seat, or low two-seater sofa can be perfect, provided the back is no higher than the footboard on the bed (or the height it would be if there were one). An ottoman, table, long stool, slatted bench, wicker settee, or even a garden seat can also look good, providing a handy spot to set down breakfast trays and newspapers.

If your bedroom is large enough, a screen is useful in front of the window or in a corner. Myriad styles are available, from fabric to Oriental lacquer, so you should be able to find something to complement your decor.

## CHARMING CHAIRS

All manner of chairs can be accommodated in the bedroom:

- **Easy chairs ranging from slipper chairs to wing chairs are the ultimate bedroom seating.**
- **The informality of wicker, cane, and rattan chairs and settees is ideal.**
- **Painted chairs with tie-on cushions look perky in country-style bedrooms.**
- **Antique or reproduction chairs look right in traditional decor.**

**RIGHT:** In this attic bedroom, a planter's chair provides low-slung seating which is in keeping with the low level of all the furniture tucked under the eaves.

# DRESSING TABLES

After the bed, the dressing table is traditionally the main focal point of a woman's bedroom. An even better reason for lavishing attention on it, however, is the pleasure it can give. Sitting at a beautiful dressing table offers a well-earned respite from a frenetic lifestyle.

Situating the dressing table at the window affords plenty of natural light. (A north-facing window is best, as the light is relatively constant and casts few shadows.) Artificial light should come from lamps placed at each side of the mirror, so the light falls evenly on your face. Lighting from behind you is not strong enough to allow you to see what you are doing.

Because dressing tables are often covered with skirts, the table underneath can be just about anything. Don't skimp on the skirt, however—it can be as simple and tailored or as frilly and feminine as you wish, so long as it creates a luxurious effect.

**FAR LEFT**: Vintage textiles, a multitude of pictures, and a pair of candle lamps flanking a large mirror set the scene for a dream dressing table.

**LEFT**: This dressing table is perfectly lit, with daylight streaming in the window.

**ABOVE**: Part of the pleasure a dressing table gives derives from the chance to sit surrounded by your favorite items, so they should be chosen and arranged with care. Here, antique books and treasured notes are displayed with fresh spring flowers.

## ON DISPLAY

Everyday beauty items can be hidden out of sight—the point of a dressing table is to display evocative treasures, such as these items:

- **Silver-capped crystal perfume bottles**
- **Silver-handled makeup brushes**
- **Tortoiseshell hairbrushes and hand mirrors**
- **Small, framed photos of family and close friends**
- **Letters tied with a ribbon**
- **A vase of fragrant flowers**

# GUEST ROOMS

A guest bedroom should be welcoming and comfortable, even if it normally does double duty as a hobby room, home office, den, or something else. Furnish it with a comfortable double bed (or pair of twins) and lovely bedding, as you would for your own bedroom. In addition, there should be two nightstands, a chest of drawers (empty), a full-length mirror, and good lighting (see page 191). If possible, create a sitting area with armchairs and an occasional table. A writing desk cum dressing table, footstool, and television would also be useful if there is room, while a small refrigerator in the closet, a coffeemaker, a telephone, and a computer hook-up would be five-star luxury. Somewhere to hang up clothes is essential, so don't fill the closet with your out-of-season clothes. If there isn't a closet, create a hanging area with a rail in an alcove or just a coat rack or some hooks on the back of the door.

**ABOVE:** When guests arrive after a long journey, you will want them to feel able to relax and enjoy themselves, and this will be much easier if their room is set up like a home from home.

**BELOW:** A sitting area with comfortable chairs is important in a guest bedroom. Guests shouldn't have to sit on the bed whenever they want some privacy.

If you use the room yourself, make sure that it's easy to convert into a guest room, with adequate storage for your own things. Work or hobbies should be put on lightweight or roll-around tables or in file cabinets on castors and quickly moved out of the way. If there's a stationary bike, put it in one corner with a screen in front of it to make it disappear. Do not let this room become an all-purpose dumping ground, or you will never have time to get it into shape just before guests arrive.

If you don't have a guest room, you will need to find a place elsewhere in the house for overnight guests to sleep, such as a curtained bed tucked into an alcove on a landing, or curtained bunk beds fitted into a hallway. If you have to use the living room or family room, a convertible bed such as a sofa bed (see page 168) will be essential, and you could perhaps adapt an armoire or nearby coat closet for guests to hang up their clothes. Think in terms of dual-purpose furnishings: a footstool that can be used as a bedside table, a blanket that becomes a throw by day. Position the sofa bed so there will still be space to move around the room when it is in use. The aim is to avoid causing major upheaval when guests come to stay, without impinging on the room's normal uses.

**BELOW:** Furnish a guest bedroom as carefully as you do your own room, with ample storage, nightstands, seating, mirrors, good lighting, and—especially— a comfortable bed.

# A HOME FROM HOME

Follow this checklist to make sure your guest room contains everything to make guests feel welcome:

- **Extra pillows and blankets or duvets**
- **Skirt hangers and padded hangers**
- **Fruit and snacks**
- **Magazines and books**
- **Maps and local information**
- **Stationery and stamps**
- **Alarm clock**
- **Hairdryer**
- **Fluffy towels**
- **Fresh flowers and scented candles**

**RIGHT:** A guest room decorated in a warm color scheme and beautifully furnished, with many thoughtful small touches, will make guests feel truly welcome in your home.

# CHILDREN'S ROOMS

Bedrooms are important personal spaces for children, where they can find interest and stimulation as well as privacy. Don't fall into the common trap of creating a baby's nursery for the new arrival. The room will be wonderful—briefly—but then, seemingly overnight, the baby will have become a preschool child who hates babyish things. A blank canvas is more versatile, with bright, cheerful fabrics and paint colors that will appeal to the very young and older children. Avoid dark or strong colors or all white—yellow is a good color on which to base a decor, particularly as it lacks gender associations. It is advisable to line curtains or shades, to help darken the room during a child's daytime naps. Wallpaper borders, lampshades, bed linen, and posters can be used to add designs of interest to the child at any age.

Where possible, the furniture, too, should be purchased with a view to the future. A diaper-changing table (with a guard to stop the baby from rolling off) could later become a dressing table or hobby table and then a desk. The feeding chair could become the child's armchair. Chests of drawers are just as suitable for diapers as for sports gear.

Older children can help pick out colors, wallpapers, or fabrics, and even help put them up, perhaps attempting simple stenciling or applying paint to a cupboard.

**RIGHT:** The painted stripes on the floor and the rest of the decor and furnishings in this room would appeal to any young girl and are unlikely to need replacing for a considerable time.

**BELOW LEFT AND BELOW:** A bed can express the child's own tastes and dreams, whether it is a platform or bunk bed (only after the age of six years) or a fantasy bed that can be a princess's castle, a boat, a train. Varying the linens allows the basic structure underneath to be used for years.

# BEDROOM FLOORS

Because bedroom floors don't receive a lot of heavy wear and because they do get walked on by bare feet, wall-to-wall carpet is popular. These days there are some irresistible textures available in natural fibers like 100 percent wool, wool with linen, and wool with sisal. These loop-pile carpets come mainly in natural colors and subtle self-patterns such as check, stripe, and herringbone. They are designed to replicate the texture of natural matting, which itself is still widely used (jute being softer underfoot than sisal, seagrass, or coir, and therefore more suitable for bedrooms). Perhaps the most luxurious-feeling carpets for bare feet are shag pile and Saxony carpets. Like loop pile, they flatten over time and so are not practical in high-use areas, where twist-pile is preferable.

A dark carpet will make a room look smaller while a light one makes it look more spacious. A light carpet shows the dirt more than a midtone or dark carpet, but this is not such a factor in a bedroom as it is in rooms where the floors receive a lot of wear.

**RIGHT:** Dark wood strip flooring looks handsome throughout the home, and sets off most color schemes. Hard flooring is especially suitable if anyone in the house suffers from allergies.

Solid-color carpets are always a safe option, and can be chosen after you have selected any patterned elements in the room. A number of attractive patterned carpets are available now, too, including plaids in lovely colors. Patterned carpet looks best in an uncluttered room that doesn't have a great deal of other pattern, but if you do combine one with another pattern, try to make sure they have at least one color in common (see pages 34–5).

Wood floors look good in the bedroom, as elsewhere, and sanded floorboards that have been bleached or painted white to allow the grain to show through seem especially suited to bedrooms. Nevertheless, they are hard and noisy, so you may want to combine them with rugs. Oriental rugs are always an attractive option, but in country-style bedrooms it's hard to improve upon the traditional braided or woven rag rug.

**ABOVE:** Oriental rugs provide rich color and pattern that look just as good in traditional styles of decor with antique furniture, as in contemporary homes with modern furnishings.

**LEFT:** White-painted floorboards add to the summery quality of this light and airy bedroom.

**ABOVE:** Spotlights and a floor lamp contribute to the lighting in this bedroom, but it's the candles in the splendid wrought-iron candelabra that create the atmosphere.

# BEDROOM LIGHTING

A bedroom needs a wide range of artificial lighting, from good bright light for applying makeup, picking out clothes, and reading, to soft atmospheric lighting for relaxing. The best sources of background lighting in bedrooms are wall lights, uplights, or table lamps. In many homes, however, a central ceiling fixture is the main light source, the harsh glare from which is very noticeable when you are lying in bed. The best solution is either to remove it entirely or to fit it with a fixture that screens the bulb. A pendant bowl, for example, is a traditional design that looks like a glass bowl hanging from three chains, and the bulb is hidden inside. A pendant bowl in a warm beige tone gives a softer light than a white one.

Good bedside lights are needed for reading in bed. The swing-arm type mounted on the wall is best—if you have a four-poster with bed hangings, you will need to have slits made in the curtains for the lights to poke through. Bedside lamps on nightstands also work well, as do floor lamps, provided they are high enough to shine on the book. They should have two-way switches at the door and bed. All bedroom lighting should be separately controlled and fitted with dimmers.

For a magical effect when you are lying in bed, star lights (tiny halogen capsules) can be scattered around the ceiling to provide bright pinpoints of light like stars.

## SEEING THE LIGHT

Make sure your bedside lamps are adequate:

- **The lower edge of the shade should be at eye level when you are sitting up in bed.**
- **The shade should prevent the light from shining right in your face.**

**BELOW:** Table and floor lamps create intimate pools of light in this romantic bedroom, as well as providing good light for reading, whether in bed or seated in the armchair.

# BATHROOMS

This most personal of spaces needs to be practical and functional for everyone in the house, while also fulfilling the role of a restorative haven in which to unwind from the stresses of the day. Bathrooms are expensive and inconvenient to replace from scratch, but fortunately there are lots of creative ways to transform the space into the restful retreat you deserve. Once you understand which materials work best in the steamy atmosphere of the bathroom, you can let your imagination run wild.

**RIGHT:** A plain white tub is transformed into a feminine haven with the use of delicate fabrics, draped in generous swags.

# BATHROOM COLORS

You are very lucky if you are starting from scratch and replacing all the fixtures, tiles, and flooring of a bathroom, because you can put together exactly the color scheme you desire. Because you are unlikely to be be changing them again soon, it's best to go for white fixtures and neutral-colored flooring and tiles. Fashions and tastes change, and these "non-colors" will stand the test of time, giving you much more scope. Also, white is the best color for fixtures if you want an old-fashioned style of bathroom, and it need not look clinical. You can still have a strong decorating scheme if you wish, as color can be lavished on untiled walls, furniture, towels, rugs, and details (see pages 200 and 206).

If you are not replacing existing tiles, you might want to consider painting over them with specialist tile paint or even tiling over them with one of the easy-to-apply tiles especially designed for layering over existing tiles. If you are choosing new tiles, consider whether their color and pattern, if any, would allow you to change the decor easily in the future. In addition to a vast choice of ceramic tiles, other exciting types of tiles are available, including mirrored, marble, bronze, and translucent glass. The latter look especially lovely teamed with the soft, shimmering colors of today's frosted glass partitions and shower cubicles.

Although tiles come in some achingly gorgeous colors which need nothing else apart from the graphic lines of white grout, many of the most beautiful effects utilize neutral or near-neutral tones. Tiny mosaic tiles in subtle shades of beige are wonderfully elegant with white fittings and a limestone floor. Alternating rows of square white ceramic tiles and rectangular dove-gray marble slips look equally sophisticated. Even plain white tiles can look stunning with tiny black diamond tiles inset at the corners; or in combination with two black-and-white checkerboard rows at eye level and a

**LEFT:** Relate the color scheme of the master bath to its bedroom, whether by using the same colors in a different pattern, as shown here, or by reversing or even contrasting the colors.

**RIGHT:** Even the smallest touches of color can have a big impact. Think through the accents you are likely to include—they can be as mundane as natural sponges and specialist soaps—and then work backward from there to decide on a color scheme.

row of black tiles at baseboard height. There is nothing more dramatic in a bathroom than black and white.

For walls that aren't tiled, use a vinyl wall covering or scrubbable paint. You could perhaps paint the walls with stripes, such as narrow, wobbly ones produced using a roller. A faux marble or woodgrain paint finish could also look fabulous, particularly if you want to extend the neutral color scheme. Stenciling is another option, as some very upscale, geometric or abstract stencil designs are available these days. Or, alternatively, you could go for wall-to-wall mirror, preferably the heated, fog-resistant type.

When a bathroom adjoins a bedroom, create continuity by relating the decor, possibly by reversing the main color and accent color. Similarly, giving a powder room the same decor as the adjoining hallway will make it seem bigger, particularly if the colors are light and if similar tones are used for the walls as for the floor. However, many people like the powder room to have an element of fun, so you could perhaps use an unusual wall covering, such as old *New Yorker* covers, or tea-stained pages of music manuscript, finished with a coat of sealer.

As always, the colors you actually use will depend on your starting point, whether that is existing fixtures, new tiles, a window treatment, or a wall covering with which you've fallen in love. Light colors will be refreshing and will make the bathroom look larger, while deep colors could be dramatic or cozy, depending on what they are combined with. Bright colors will be cheerful and energizing, and great to wake up to each morning.

## DISTRACTION TECHNIQUES

If you are not replacing fixtures but you dislike the color, simply draw attention away from them:

- **Paint or replace bath paneling (or paint the outside of a clawfoot tub).**
- **Fit a vanity or skirt around a sink; box in a cistern.**
- **Change the window and shower curtains.**
- **If existing fixtures are pastel, bring in stronger or brighter colors. If existing fixtures are bright, introduce calm colors and bright details.**

# BATHROOM FLOORS

Bathroom flooring needs to be waterproof and nonslip. Resilient floor coverings —vinyl, linoleum, cork, or rubber—are good in bathrooms, and come in both tile and sheet form. Vinyl is easy to clean and quite soft to walk on, especially the cushioned variety. It is available in solid colors, patterns, and copies of other materials including wood, limestone, terrazzo, and brick. Linoleum has similar qualities to vinyl. Cork, too is warm, soft, and quiet underfoot; it usually comes presealed. Even warmer, softer, and quieter, rubber is available in a range of colors; both the studded and the ribbed finishes are nonslip. Wood flooring is not suitable but you could use a laminate, which has a wood-effect vinyl surface and is waterproof.

Flooring-weight mosaic tiles look lovely. Terra-cotta and quarry tiles, which are unglazed, have to be sealed to make them waterproof. Glazed ceramic tiles, which come in beautiful colors and patterns, can be used if they have a slip-resistant finish, but they are cold and hard underfoot. This also applies to thin stone tiles. Marble looks great but is cold and slippery. Terrazzo (polished marble and granite chips in a cement base) is handsome and fairly nonslip. However, terrazzo, and also terra-cotta, quarry and glazed ceramic tiles, should ideally be laid on concrete, which precludes upstairs bathrooms. Carpet is difficult to keep clean and dry—choose mats and rugs instead.

**RIGHT:** As well as providing a practical, waterproof solution, hard flooring reflects the light, and has the effect of seeming to "push the walls out." This can make smaller bathrooms look more spacious.

**FAR RIGHT:** Floors offer a great opportunity to add color to a bathroom. These tiles give the room a warm, cozy feel.

# BATH STORAGE

Bathrooms are expected to accommodate an enormous amount of personal-care implements and products, yet most bathrooms have only minimal storage space. With a little thought, however, it should be possible to hide away everything except items that are worthy of being on show. (For how to deal with these, see pages 200–1.)

The most common storage piece is the medicine cabinet, and versions are available that incorporate fog-resistant mirrors, shaver points, and lights. Small old cupboards and glass-fronted cabinets also make attractive medicine cabinets.

Built-in cabinets are the most deluxe and space-efficient form of bathroom storage. The most familiar of these is the vanity cupboard, but often there is room for more built-ins. A whole wall of cabinets is sheer luxury. Sometimes, however, they can look too regimented and soulless. As with kitchen cabinets, changing the knobs (perhaps to leather or rope straps, cut-glass knobs, or stainless steel bars) might improve the look. Glass-fronted cabinets usually look more interesting than those with solid doors, and some cabinets can be covered completely with mirror. If the doors of your old cabinets have recessed panels, you could possibly replace the panels with fabric or wire mesh. Built-in cabinets can be constructed so as to look old-fashioned, and if you are remodeling a bathroom, you might want to break up the expanse of doors by building them either side of a clawfoot tub that projects out into the room.

Large freestanding pieces of old furniture—armoires, wardrobes, dressers, bookcases, even pie safes—provide handsome and capacious bathroom storage if you have the floor space. Similarly, a vintage sideboard, chest of drawers, or marble-topped washstand could be adapted for use as a vanity by having a sink inset into the top. Old chests of apothecary drawers are invaluable for organizing everything from toothpaste tubes to combs and hairbrushes.

Spaces that are usually wasted can sometimes be used, too: Build a door or pull-out drawer in the bath paneling, or replace a chair with a stool or window seat that has a hinged lid. Whatever storage you create, remember that medicines and cleaning materials should be in lockable cupboards if there are ever any children in the house.

**ABOVE:** This unusual piece of furniture provides a display area as well as drawer space. If freestanding furniture looms up too large in a bathroom, painting it a light color brings it back down to comfortable proportions.

**THROW IN THE TOWEL**

Baskets of all shapes and sizes provide attractive places to keep clean towels, though they may need to be lined with quilted fabric to protect the contents from being snagged on sharp ends. A row of small sisal baskets matching your color scheme looks lovely on a shelf.

**CUPBOARD LOVE**

Freestanding furniture makes a bathroom look like a "real" room. If you have the space, an old-fashioned wardrobe fitted with shelves and mirrors offers unbeatable storage space. A linen press, chest of drawers, armoire, or other piece of case furniture could be used in a similar way.

# BATHROOM ACCESSORIES

If your bathroom fixtures, tiles, and flooring are white or other neutral tones, the accessories are your opportunity to add color and atmosphere. Anything ugly should be stored out of sight (see page 198), leaving the display space to bath oils in nice bottles, crystals in glass jars, colored soaps, scented candles, perfume bottles, natural sponges and loofahs, wooden-handled back brushes and nail brushes, ceramic soap dishes, colored drinking glasses, and anything else you deem beautiful and functional.

Obviously these will need to be displayed in such a way that they look uncontrived and uncluttered, and don't get in the way. Suitable surfaces include wooden shelves in a piece of furniture, or shelves above a vanity unit; glass shelves stretched across a window or niche, or in a corner; windowsills and the narrow shelf on top of wainscoting; tiled ledges over boxed-in plumbing or a boxed-in tub; wicker shelves and tiered stands; individual wooden cubbyholes mounted on the wall; or small pieces of furniture such as an antique wine table, whatnot, or dumbwaiter.

The walls can be brought into service, too. Back brushes and shower gels will hang from hooks, and a Shaker-style peg rail will hold everything from drawstring bags to

**RIGHT:** A simple tray holds feminine accessories, creating an informal "dressing table" in a bathroom where space is limited.

## HOLDING FORTH

Attractive containers help to make the most of your accessories:

- Sit fancy soaps on a porcelain cake stand in the powder room.
- Hold wooden brushes in a little zinc bucket.
- Stand loofahs and sponges together in a wooden pail with rope handle.
- Roll up guest towels tightly and place them side by side in a basket or a small wrought iron wine rack.

mirrors and candle lanterns. If there's room, you could also include some framed pictures on the walls, and near a wall you could place a large plant stand or garden urn containing a plant that will thrive in the subtropical conditions.

Finally, the most important "accessories" for the bathroom, in terms of both practicality and color, are the towels. Towels in use need to have somewhere they can quickly and easily be hung up properly. A towel warmer is ideal, particularly as it means your towels will always be lovely and warm when you use them. A quilt rack or an antique iron rail makes an attractive towel holder—or you could, of course, use a conventional chrome towel bar. You also need shelves to keep folded clean towels, not only to have them handy when needed but also because of their contribution to the color scheme of the room. Some towel bars are designed to hold a stack of folded towels on top, and two or three rows of hanging towels underneath. Otherwise, some of the deeper shelves mentioned above could be used.

**ABOVE:** Never underestimate the power of soap! Pretty soaps are a simple and inexpensive addition to a bathroom, but they bring a welcome splash of color, as well as a pleasing scent.

**RIGHT:** A wire hanging rack is a practical and safe way to store glass bottles and other breakables, especially if you have to stretch up to reach them. The high decorative "fence" around the shelf acts as a safety barrier and also looks attractive.

# SMALL BATHROOMS

Most people's bathrooms are smaller than they would like, and now that sybaritic bathing is on the increase, the size limitations are all the more pronounced. However, even if you cannot borrow some space from an adjoining room, you can still make a bathroom seem more spacious and help it accommodate your needs. Your options fall into two categories: structural changes and cosmetic changes.

Among the structural possibilities: ● Remove the shower cubicle and tray, and turn the whole room into a wet room, which uses Venetian plaster to create a hermetically sealed unit that is completely leakproof. ● Replace the shower door so that it opens inward to save space. ● Replace the fixtures with smaller or differently shaped versions, such as a triangular or square tub (bearing in mind that it may be deeper than a regular bath) or a corner sink. Remember to allow at least 30 inches in front of each fixture for using it. A freestanding, clawfoot tub increases the feeling of space because you can see underneath it. ● Build in some additional storage space to swallow up all the bathroom clutter that's getting in the way.

Of the cosmetic alterations, the most drastic is to retile if you think the pattern is making the room look too confined. Less drastic strategies: ● Paint the tiles rather than removing them (see page 194). ● Declutter and make sure you are getting full use out of existing storage space. ● Mirror the walls (if possible with heated glass, so they won't steam up). ● If the wall color is strong or dark, change it to a light, cool, airy tone. ● If the curtains are heavy or are obscuring part of the window, replace them with translucent curtains or shades.

## OPENING UP

Create a feeling of spaciousness by removing barriers:

- **Open the bathroom partially to the bedroom, replacing the wall with glass bricks or a frosted glass screen to let in more light.**
- **A solid door could be replaced with frosted glass.**
- **The window could perhaps be enlarged.**

**LEFT:** Space is maximized in this simple yet stylish master bathroom. The light, neutral color scheme makes it look more spacious.

**RIGHT:** A space-saving corner sink and a display shelf are tucked well out of the way under the eaves, making the most of every inch of space.

**STAR TURN**

A pretty shower curtain will turn a bathtub in an alcove into a dramatic stage set. Even the wall can become an illusionistic backdrop, with trompe l'oeil decoration. A valance can be added using an ordinary valance rod mounted on the ceiling in front of the shower curtain, as here. Or, if the shower bar is lower than the ceiling, the valance could be attached with grommets and shower curtain hooks to the front channel of a dual-channel shower bar, and the curtain and its liner to the back channel.

# SHOWER CURTAINS

Because of all the hard surfaces in a bathroom, fabric becomes even more important, not only to soften the room visually but also to deaden sound. Although shower curtains are often made of specialist plastic fabric, they can instead consist of a regular fabric exterior plus an inner plastic liner, and so they offer an excellent opportunity to simultaneously add color, pattern, softness, femininity, and improved acoustics to the bathroom.

The fabric should be washable, tightly woven, and lightweight but strong. It shouldn't have a glazed or polished finish on which water splashes could leave a mark. The curtain is made in the same way as a normal unlined curtain, but it needs to be the same size as the liner. They usually have grommets inserted along the top, in exactly the same place in both the curtain and the liner, and are hooked together to the shower bar with special shower curtain hooks. The curtain hangs outside the tub and the liner inside. The shower curtain for a freestanding clawfoot tub is often hung from a round metal hoop suspended from the ceiling above the tub, and the curtain drapes over the sides of the tub.

Instead of grommets at the top, tabs or ties could be used. In that case, a dual-channel shower bar would be used. This has two separate tracks, allowing the curtain and liner to slide independently. Curtains can include contrasting borders on the leading and lower edges, ties at the leading edges to fasten the curtains together, and washable trimmings such as rickrack or ribbon, so there is every opportunity to have the best-dressed tub in town.

**RIGHT:** Ethereal curtains with check binding are neatly tied together, providing a suitably feminine surround for a dainty clawfoot tub.

# NOSTALGIC BATHROOMS

Despite the glamour of the very latest whirlpool tubs and multihead shower massages, many people prefer old-fashioned bathrooms with gleaming white fixtures and dark wood. In pride of place is the large, freestanding, enamelled cast-iron clawfoot tub, with splendid brass or chrome plumbing designed to be seen in all its glory. A variation is the clawfoot slipper tub, which is higher at one end to make long soaks in the bath even more comfortable. Clawfoot tubs are traditionally white, but the outside can be painted, which sets off the beautiful rounded rim nicely.

Perfect companions for one of these tubs are a white ceramic console sink or large pedestal sink fitted with a traditionally styled faucet, and a white high-tank toilet with mahogany seat. The fixtures are available from salvage companies, but excellent reproduction versions are also available, complete with modern technology hidden from view. Finish the effect with a mahogany highboy or wardrobe in which to store towels and bathroom clutter; an easy chair; a magnificent mirror over the sink; a towel warmer, and a small bookcase to hold essential bathroom reading.

If you have standard white bathroom fixtures you can create a similar effect by replacing the paneling around the tub with mahogany panels, replacing the faucets on the bath and sink with traditionally styled versions, and fitting a new mahogany seat on the toilet. For an authentic look, tiles and flooring should be black and white.

The light fixtures can blend in with the nostalgic ambience, but must still be useful. Recessed halogen downlights will provide a safe, sparkly white light for general lighting, while two enclosed wall lights flanking the mirror will provide a good light at the sink area.

**RIGHT:** White vitreous enamel and dark wood create a dramatic setting for bathing in style and luxury.

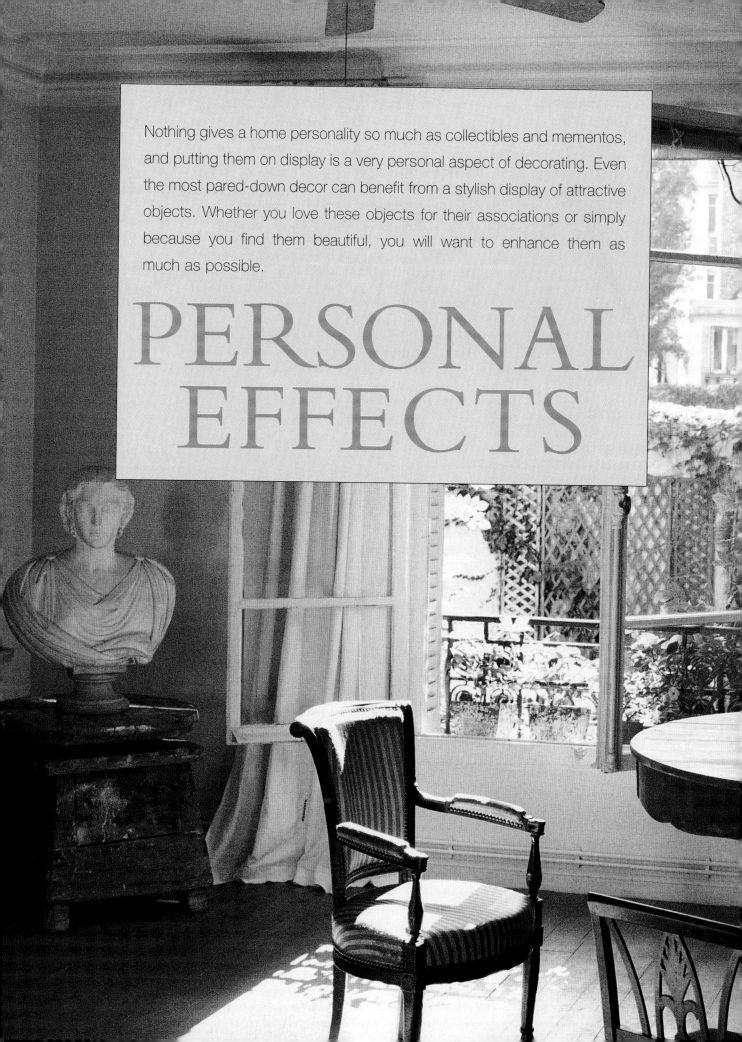

Nothing gives a home personality so much as collectibles and mementos, and putting them on display is a very personal aspect of decorating. Even the most pared-down decor can benefit from a stylish display of attractive objects. Whether you love these objects for their associations or simply because you find them beautiful, you will want to enhance them as much as possible.

# PERSONAL EFFECTS

**LEFT:** A variety of baskets are tucked under a cabinet on a countertop, with more baskets inside the cabinet, providing an interesting display that also can be used for storage in this workroom.

**RIGHT:** A large collection of straw hats on the wall of an adjacent room makes an amusing display.

**BELOW RIGHT:** Placing these small collectibles on the console table in the entry hall means that they can be seen by every visitor. The table lamp will shed light on the collection at night.

## IN THE LIMELIGHT

Special lighting can enhance collections:

- **Position downlights or tracklights so the beams shine directly on a collection arranged on a table.**
- **Aim downlights or tracklights at groups of pictures. They can also be used to illuminate individual pictures.**
- **Place a collection of silver-topped crystal sugar dredgers or scent bottles on triangular glass shelves in a corner. Fit downlights above them and uplights beneath to maximize the sparkly display.**

# IDEAS FOR COLLECTIONS

A collection can be any group, large or small, of items that have something in common, such as material (Bakelite, perhaps), type (for example, silver-topped crystal bottles), theme (nautical, equestrian), motif (hens, bees), style (Shaker, art deco), period (Victorian, 1960's), or color (such as red, black, and white).

Even the most mundane objects can take on a new appeal simply by being part of a group. For the grouped display to look good, be prepared to impose order on the arrangement, making sure there is a good balance (but not rigid symmetry) and a variety in size, height, and shape of the objects. If the collection is large and unwieldy, you might need to remove some of the less interesting pieces, and possibly introduce some whimsical, amusing, or intriguing ones.

Display the collection against a contrasting background, and consider the distance and angle the items should be viewed from. Enamel boxes, for example,

will benefit from being seen at close range and from above, such as on a tabletop. Viewed from across a room, game boards might look best on a wall, and a collection of trivets, trays, and platters would look dramatic in a plate rack.

It's more interesting if the function of the items on display relates to that of the room. For example, tortoiseshell combs and wooden-backed hand mirrors could be stuck to the bathroom wall with adhesive mirror pads, wooden breadboards displayed on a shelf in the kitchen, or vintage metal watering cans lined up on a shelf in the sun porch. An old pair of shoe lasts could be hung on a bedroom wall to serve as unusual hooks.

# DISPLAYING GLASS

With its myriad reflections and glorious sparkle, glass really does bring a room to life, whether it is the shining transparency of clear glass, the delicate intricacy of engraved glass, the deep facets of cut glass, the robust commemorative ware of pressed glass, the shimmering vibrancy of colored glass, or a combination of all of these. For maximum impact, place your glass pieces close together on a shelf or table, positioning the tallest one about a third of the way in from one side.

## SHINING THROUGH

Glass brings a room to life, especially if you follow some of these tips:

- **Glass vases and dishes look wonderful filled with shells, silver cake-decoration balls, dragées (silver sugared almonds), marbles, or glass droplets from old chandeliers.**
- **Use glass on shelves or in a cabinet to brighten up a gloomy corner.**
- **A dark velvet lining in a cabinet shows glass off to perfection.**
- **To light a display of glass, or other items, a down-light set into the ceiling above it is very effective.**
- **For a truly sensational effect, place cranberry glass in a window against the leafy view outside.**

**LEFT**: Sizes, shapes, colors and styles mix happily in a collection of glassware, but a theme creates a more unified look. This collection of antique lamps shows how pieces of different sizes can work together.

**ABOVE**: A window provides the traditional backlit display area for glass, where it can sparkle in the sun's rays. Fit glass shelves into the window recess or window frame, or place the pieces on the windowsill or a table in front of it.

# DISPLAYING CERAMICS

Ceramics are among the most versatile of all collectibles. Whether you display decorative china or the tableware that you use every day, they make a colorful and infinitely varied arrangement. They are also the perfect form of wall display for the kitchen because they are not affected by steam, unlike some pictures. Even a shelf full of neatly stacked plates and dishes can look decorative, particularly if interspersed with pitchers and tureens.

Whatever decorative style of ceramic you collect, from spongeware or slipware to lusterware or Sèvres porcelain, a display will look better if you don't juxtapose porcelain and pottery, which go together like chalk and cheese! Made from highly glazed fine white china clay and china stone, porcelain is fired at high temperatures. It is always translucent and has a hard, smooth finish. Bone china is an English type of porcelain that contains bone ash as well as china clay. When pottery, which is clay-based, is made non-porous through firing at a high temperature, it is known as stoneware; all other pottery is called earthenware and is glazed to make it non-porous.

The safest place to display valuable porcelain is behind glass in a china cabinet, but ceramics also look great on a hutch, in a corner cupboard, on a plate rack, on a narrow, high shelf that runs around the room, sitting on a stand or simply sitting on a tabletop or windowsill, or hung on the wall.

**RIGHT:** With its fabulous array of ceramics, this dining room provides ample proof of the variety and versatility of this collectible.

**BELOW LEFT:** The perfect combination: ceramics that are linked by common factors—the maker, the basic style, and the color palette—but have sufficient contrast of height, shape, individual color, and pattern to make a stunning display.

## POT LUCK

Try one of these eye-catching displays:

- **A plate rack in which each shelf holds plates of a different size, shape, and color, corresponding to your color scheme**
- **Creamware with pierced rims on a dark wooden hutch**
- **A line of matching teacups, planted with spring bulbs**
- **Lusterware plates hanging on the wall around a gilded wall bracket holding a lusterware bowl**

# DISPLAYING OLD BOOKS

Old books look wonderful anywhere. The craftsmanship and tactile qualities of their leather bindings and gilt tooling make them irresistible even before you open the covers. Add to that the joy of collecting books you love, possibly with exquisite illustrations and marbled endpapers, and it's not surprising that old books, whether or not they are valuable first editions, hold such a fascination for collectors and decorators alike. Vellum-bound books are also highly prized. Though the texts themselves (often treatises on astronomy, science, and religion) are unlikely to be read, the creamy color of the binding looks amazing among other old books and antiques.

Old books look fabulous mixed with china, glassware, and small sculptures because their rectilinear shape, texture, and somber colors contrast so beautifully with curves, smooth surfaces, and delicate tones.

**ABOVE AND LEFT:** Break up regimented lines in bookcases with stacks of books, small framed pictures, and vases of pretty flowers.

**LEFT:** Even just a few old books look good as part of a still life with glass and ceramics, and antique vellum-bound books are a decorator's dream.

## GOOD BOOK KEEPING

Old books make great displays:

- **Stack them to form mini-plinths for pieces of china and vases of flowers.**
- **Open some of them to show off interesting illustrations.**

- **Combine them with book-related antiques like bookmarks or paper-cutters.**
- **Juxtapose them with antique ivory and bone, or with creamy glassware such as striped white and clear glass.**

# COLLECTIONS IN THE HOME

Collections of favorite objects, treasures, travel souvenirs, and other mementos are the most personal part of a home, giving a room character and individuality. Not only do collections offer you a chance to surround yourself with things you love, but they embody your taste. Collections can be used to underline your color scheme while simultaneously preventing a room from looking either too bland or too "designed." You may even be able to use the collection as the basis of the whole decor.

If you are an avid collector, you risk having too much of a good thing by allowing the collections to take over a room (or even the whole home). Collections should never disrupt the function of a room—for example, usurping tabletops where drinks, lamps, and reading material need to be placed. Nor should they dominate the room so that it starts looking more like a museum than a home. Make sure that you can detach yourself and scrutinize the displays, and their overall effect, with the eye of a dispassionate decorator.

If you have just one very large display, consider whether it would look better split into two or perhaps simply reduced in size. If you have several collections on show in the same room, make sure that the eye will glide smoothly between them, from one area of interest to another.

**BELOW:** Virtually every decorative item in this room is part of a collection, yet each arrangement is so carefully controlled that it is a delight to behold.

## EYE OF THE BEHOLDER

With restraint, collections can be built into the very fabric of a home:

- **Instead of regarding every flat surface as yet another opportunity to set out a collection, look for surfaces that are ideally suited to the nature of the objects you are displaying.**
- **Avoid having a lot of similar collections and try to display them in different ways.**
- **Take great care arranging each aesthetically.**
- **If you are building a display area such as a bookcase or shelving in a niche, try to include integrated accent lighting.**

**ABOVE:** Americana is used throughout this Colonial-style home, but the displays are so harmonious and varied that the Colonial theme never becomes labored.

# SMALL COLLECTIONS

A collection doesn't have to be large to have impact. Often, a small, well-arranged collection will make a stronger impression than a large, sprawling one. Even a group of just a few select pieces qualifies as a "collection" and, if well displayed, can be the most charming focal point in a room.

Give each object "breathing space" to show off its shape and to allow it to have maximum impact. Include odd numbers of items in displays: As every flower arranger knows, an arrangement consisting of three elements is more dynamic and interesting than one made up of two or four, because the symmetry inherent in even numbers creates too static an effect.

**ABOVE:** A simple tray holds a small collection of lamps tightly together as a centerpiece for a long dining table. More lamps are mounted on the window frame.

**FAR LEFT:** With its candlestick and its linen cloth arranged over the corner of the table, this understated but still carefully arranged shell display is perfectly balanced.

**LEFT:** A collection of lovely old tiles has been laid on a tabletop to provide a suitably delicate backdrop for a clay pot holding flowers and a wire basket of eggs. The louvered shutter and small china tureen add to the range of wonderful textures and colors.

## SELECT FEW

Even a tiny collection of objects can make a visual statement:

- **Antique garden tools have such unusual shapes that a small collection is instantly intriguing.**
- **A few African masks hung on the wall would have quite enough impact for most living rooms.**
- **Three intricate cross-stitch samplers make a stunning wall grouping.**
- **Even just a few colored glass plates look dramatic in a window with light streaming through.**

# ECLECTIC COLLECTIONS

An eclectic collection encompasses objects from different styles and periods that are linked in some other way, such as pattern or texture. Sometimes the common denominator is so subtle as to be virtually undetectable, in which case "eclectic display" would be a more accurate description.

Unexpected or incongruous juxtapositions, often with more than a little playfulness underlying them, are what make eclectic collections so lively. Amusing, witty, or intriguing contrasts may be set up within the predominantly harmonious arrangement, making it doubly enjoyable—contrasts, after all, are more stimulating than harmony.

Among the most enjoyable of these groupings are those where something grand is juxtaposed with something frivolous. Combinations of the antique with the modern have a similar appeal and are popular among decorators today. Ultimately, however, the most successful groupings, even if they are mischievous and flippant, have an intrinsic

## HIT THE WALL

Try these ideas for displaying eclectic collections:

- **Build a wall shelf unit comprising a series of large cubbyholes, and fill each with varying numbers of items of a particular type, such as wooden boxes, a brass weighing scale, or honey-colored vases. The contents of each cubbyhole should be similar in color but otherwise different, to contrast while looking balanced.**
- **When hanging a picture and a china plate or other dissimilar items one above the other on the wall, suspend them from the same silk picture sash.**
- **Collect items that are components of something else, such as brass weights from scales, a lid, or an architectural molding, and use them in displays of more conventional items.**

**LEFT:** A stone mantelpiece contains a variety of items, based around the blue and white color theme. By staggering the line-up and overlapping shapes, the group has been made more cohesive and interesting.

**ABOVE:** An assortment of sparkling colored and clear glassware is linked simply by the fact that it is all glass. However, the flowers in the vases and the floral-patterned fabric and wallpaper behind the display create another unifying factor.

harmony that makes the items work well together, no matter how disparate they are. The juxtaposition brings out the best qualities of each item in the collection.

Eclectic groupings tend to require more effort to get right, but that's not to say they should be avoided. It's just a matter of studying a wide variety of potential objects from different periods, and training your eye to look for the underlying shape, texture, pattern, and scale of each. These characteristics will determine how well each item relates to the others in the group.

Make a point of looking closely at eclectic collections and displays in books, magazines, homes that you particularly admire, and even restaurants. Analyze the groupings you feel are most successful, the ones you

**LEFT:** A masculine-looking display centered around a drinks tray is unified by the use of silver, in the candlesticks, tray, ice bucket, and stack of boxes.

**RIGHT:** Curved shapes are the common element in this display. Even the carved design in the fireplace echoes this theme, while the straight lines of the mantelpiece provide an effective contrast. The prevalent cool blues and violets add to the gently harmonious atmosphere.

**BELOW:** An eclectic array of pink, white, and blue-green items sits on a shelf above chairs slipcovered in the same colors, creating a fresh, feminine look.

prefer, the ones that don't work well—and why. Follow your instincts, and trust your eye, since a sense of fun and adventure is at the heart of this approach.

When you are creating an eclectic collection or display, err on the side of including fewer items in the group. Trying to cram in too much is one of the fundamental mistakes beginners make, so learn to recognize when to stop.

If an item makes an incredibly strong visual statement on its own, it will probably be difficult to incorporate into a group, as it is likely to dominate. Instead, treat it as a feature item in its own right.

# VIGNETTES

Probably the most delightful aspect of interior decorating, vignettes are intimate little still lifes within the larger context of the room—visual treats that catch the eye and allow it to linger with pure pleasure. These three-dimensional compositions can be placed on any surface and made up of virtually anything, such as sculptures, china or glassware, framed pictures, lamps or candlesticks, boxes or books, clocks, flowering plants, watering cans, pebbles, driftwood, textiles…the list is endless. What's important is that the items in the vignette look terrific together. Start with something you love, and find other objects that relate well visually, remembering always to aim for variety and balance.

**BELOW:** Try to imagine this vignette without one of the elements, and you realize how crucial each is. Without the darker mass of the screen, the display would look insipid; without the hatbox or clock, there would be too many vertical elements; without the silver vase, the vignette would lack sparkle; without the lamp, its backbone would be missing; without the shawl, it would be too hard-edged.

**RIGHT:** The shape of this chair and the outline of the watering can echo the framed drawing, while the flowering plant and books anchor the vignette, giving it just the right amount of substance.

# FRAMING & HANGING

Framed pictures always personalize a room, from a single handsome painting over a fireplace to a grouping on the wall to which everyone gravitates. Oil paintings are usually given a heavier molding than watercolors, pastels, or drawings. Traditionally, oils are framed without glass or a mat, while most artworks on paper need the "breathing space" of a mat and the protection of glass. The mat will look best if it is a different width than the frame. If the mat is light, avoid making it brighter than the whites in the picture; if it's dark, don't allow it to be darker than the blacks in the picture.

Two pictures of the same size and framed identically look good side by side. If they are different sizes, hang one above the other (whichever way you think they look better). Grouping three pictures together looks good, too, either in a vertical stack or with each at a different height but quite close together.

Hanging a group of pictures can be tricky, so try it out first on the floor—measure the spaces between the pictures, and then mark the positions on the wall. There are lots of ways to arrange pictures, depending on their number and size and on the room. If there are an even number of equal-sized pictures, you could hang them all the same distance apart, in rows of identical size. Pictures can also be placed in a single row, with

**BELOW LEFT:** Empty frames of different sizes make a strong design statement overlapping each other and leaning against the wall. Use less linear items, like the flowers and bowls here, to soften the rectilinear lines.

**BELOW:** An antique textile bearing an impressive embroidered monogram is beautiful framed in a gilt molding and hung from a white ribbon. The ridged paneling adds to the textural contrast.

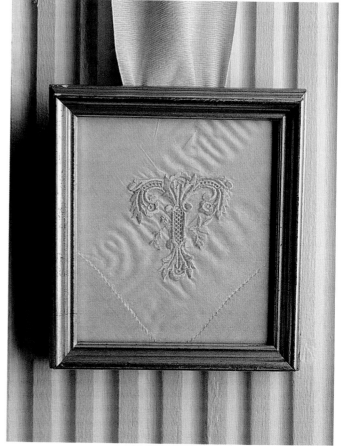

## PICTURE PERFECT

Try these ideas to make the most of your framed pictures:

- **Hang a frame with hidden wire and nail, then make it appear to be hanging on a snazzy ribbon from a decorative picture nail.**
- **Instead of a mat, use ribbon and rickrack (zigzag braid) around a picture within the frame.**
- **Hang a line of small pictures in alternating round or rectangular frames on each side of a large mirror or fireplace.**

all the top edges or all the bottom edges even with an imaginary horizontal line. Or place them within a triangle or an inverted triangle, with the smallest pictures near the point.

Yet another approach is the rectangular grouping, in which the largest pictures, or those with dark mats, are placed at the corners of the imaginary rectangle, and either a small picture with a very wide mat, or a large picture, in the center; smaller pictures are used to fill in, so that the outer edges touch the perimeter of the imaginary rectangle.

**ABOVE:** More than 40 framed family photographs make up this corner picture gallery in a living room. Most of the pictures are framed in light wood frames with cream mats, but a few have black frames to add visual interest.

Keep your home looking stylish and interesting with temporary transformations—whether you want to decorate the dining area for a special day, alter the decor to suit the season, or simply make a change to suit your mood. The beauty of these changes is that they can be made quickly and then undone as you please.

# QUICK CHANGES

# TABLE SETTINGS

As the focal point of the dining area, the table setting is part of the room's decor—but, unlike most other aspects of the decorating theme, it is constantly changing. Setting the table in a variety of different ways is half the fun of entertaining. It gives you the chance to bring out your favorite things and dream up new ideas for using them and to create a special mood. The basic elements—table linen, tableware, glasses, and flatware—can be set off in imaginative ways. Building up more than one set of some of these items obviously gives you more scope, but it's not essential. Whatever entertaining you do, a dash of drama will help create a sense of occasion. If the style of your accoutrements is in keeping with the room decor, dressing things up for a special dinner will be easy.

These days, unmatched sets of china or glass, also known as harlequin sets, are very chic. They can look charming, provided that they have some sort of link, such as being in the same color or combination of colors. They also provide flexibility when you are devising a new table setting. Harlequin sets, often created over time through occasional fleamarket purchases, are ideal for casual suppers and relaxed dinner parties. For a similar effect, you could buy tableware in one pattern but in two or more toning colors.

There is still nothing nicer than sitting down to a meal at a candlelit table sparkling with crystal and silver. It's the perfect way of making an occasion or celebration feel truly special. If you are considering investing in new china, glassware, silverware, or table linen, keep in mind the following factors. Of all the constituents of the formal dinner table, the china will have the biggest impact. Porcelain is the finest, but both porcelain and bone china are beautifully translucent and elegant. Some of the original patterns are still in production, but many contemporary patterns are equally timeless in their appeal. Classic plain white china, with or without a gold rim, and in styles ranging from delicate to more chunky, offers the greatest versatility. Unpatterned china with a colored border and a gold rim is also versatile, or you could choose a set with different-colored borders. Patterned china, though often extremely decorative, offers less scope for varying the look.

Some crystal designs have been in production for centuries. At a formal dinner, each place will have three glasses: The glass for red wine is rounder and slightly larger than the glass for white wine, which has a taller stem, and the water glass is a little larger still. The glassware that has the most clarity and weight is "full lead crystal," which contains

## TURNING THE TABLES

Ring the changes in your table settings without having to buy new tableware, glasses, or flatware:

- **Change the table linen, using homespun checks, wide stripes, Fortuny pleats, a Madras plaid, or tribal cotton.**
- **Combine a jewel-colored tapestry undercloth with a washable top cloth in a contrasting color.**
- **Put a fingerbowl by each place and float a gerbera or other spectacular flower in it.**
- **Sprinkle flower petals, crystal chandelier droplets, or silver dragées (silver sugared almonds) around the tablecloth.**

**RIGHT:** Filmy fabric wrapped around the chair backs and tied in place dresses up these dining chairs for a formal dinner.

30 percent lead and is often hand blown. "Lead crystal" contains 25 percent lead. Glassware is often decorated by cutting facets in the surface—making it sparkle like diamonds—or by engraving, gilding, or hand-painting with enamel paints. Wine connoisseurs, however, prefer plain, uncolored glass so that they can fully appreciate the wine. Nevertheless, beautiful colored glasses can be irresistible, so why not use them for the water glasses? Tableware, too, is available in gorgeous glass.

Silverware, whether sterling or silverplate, is also still produced in centuries-old designs (such as Dubarry and Old English) as well as in stunning modern shapes. It's the perfect complement to china and crystal. Echo it with more silver, such as napkin rings, a wine bucket, and salt cellars. A charger—sometimes known as an underplate, in silver, china, or glass, as well as brass or pewter—can remain at each place between courses.

## SMALL ADDS

Accessories like these add a lot to a table:

- Horn, bone, or mother-of-pearl pepper grinders
- Placecards made from shells, small candles, sugar grapes, or laurel leaves with gold writing
- Napkin rings made from glittery bracelets or sprigs of flowers

**TOP RIGHT:** Antique lead-free Venetian glass may be difficult to find in matching sets, but single items make wonderful centerpieces.

**TOP FAR RIGHT:** This exquisite candy-striped sherbet set and pitcher are made from hand-blown glass in the Venetian style.

**BOTTOM RIGHT:** Many modern manufacturers produce beautiful glass in the traditional Venetian style.

**BOTTOM FAR RIGHT:** China decorated with nature-inspired patterns adds summery cheer all year round.

A wood table makes a lovely background for china, crystal, and silver, and heat-resistant placemats will protect the surface. However, a tablecloth and matching napkins offer an excellent way to introduce more color and texture. Place a heat- and water-resistant pad the same size as the table underneath the cloth. Crisply starched white damask is traditional, but lace and plain or embroidered linen are good alternatives, and a runner down the middle of the table can look good on its own or with a tablecloth. Finish off the formal table with flowers and candles (see pages 242–4).

For casual entertaining and everyday meals, you'll need stoneware plates and bowls, which will be stronger than earthenware, plain wine glasses (the all-purpose tulip shape will suffice for both red and white wine), and stainless steel flatware. Flatware with acrylic resin or mother-of-pearl handles looks particularly decorative. Stylish placemats complete the look, with matching or contrasting napkins.

**LEFT:** A lavish table setting will transform even a small table in a living room into a table fit for a king.

# FLOWERS & PLANTS

Flowers and potted plants bring nature indoors and the country into the heart of the city, adding wonderful color and scent to the home. At the heart of their appeal is their ephemeral nature; we enjoy them all the more because their perfection is so short-lived. Like less transitory furnishings, they add not just color but texture, form, and scale as well; unlike those objects, they also add life.

Flowers are welcoming, and a large, high-impact arrangement will help to draw visitors into a room. However, dotting the room with lots of other flowers would be visually confusing. Similarly, a stunning centerpiece can be the focal point of a dining table, but there is no need to fill the dining room with flowers, which would only compete for attention with the main display.

Flower arranging is an art in itself, and there are many different approaches, ranging from the highly structured formal arrangements of florists' flowers to single stems in a sleek glass vase. Fashions in floral arts come and go, so the best approach, as always, is to follow your instincts and let your own eye be the judge. Whether you like simple posies of wildflowers or bold and exotic hothouse blooms, the chances are your taste in flowers will harmonize beautifully with your taste in interiors.

One of the most appealing styles to have grown popular over recent years is the large, informal bouquet made up of freshly picked seasonal garden flowers, foliage, berries, and branches. The best examples look as if they had just been gathered in armfuls from the garden and stuck straight into a pitcher or vase—though their unstudied elegance is usually not as artless as it appears.

**RIGHT:** When planning an arrangement, take into account its position in the room. These salmon-pink roses are set off to perfection by the wall color, and the shape of the arrangement is low enough not to obscure the reflection of the stairway in the mirror.

**BELOW:** Flowering potted plants are an invaluable backup to cut flowers, particularly in winter. Use them to create a focal point in a room or add color in a dark corner.

## IT'S A WRAP

Witty containers add an element of fun as well as color to a room:

- **Shorten the stems of bright-colored anemones and place in a water-filled glass. Wrap large laurel leaves around the glass to cover it completely, tying them in place with gold wire.**
- **Shorten the stems of some tulips and place them in a small glass vase. Wrap vividly colored raffia around the vase, and then place the whole thing inside a slightly bigger vase of the same shape.**

**BELOW:** Houseplants with strong, sculptural shapes and exotic flowers are ideal for contemporary homes. They are particularly well suited to the wide open spaces of converted warehouses and lofts.

**RIGHT:** Blooms in two vivid shades of pink make a spectacular centerpiece in this neutral-toned dining room, though ideally the arrangement should be a little lower so as not to interrupt sight lines.

**LEFT:** The white flowers of viburnum make a lovely informal display in any decorating scheme.

**RIGHT:** Orchids in a variety of containers, including a tureen, are massed beneath a large portrait, making this area rather than the table the focal point of the room.

**BELOW:** A dark vase sets off these salmon-pink roses beautifully. Synonymous with summer, roses are for many people the perfect flower.

## GOOD MIXER

The flowers of the guelder-rose (*Viburnum opulus* "Roseum," also known as the snowball bush or European cranberry bush), which are a soft lime green before they open to white, are a gift to flower arrangers. Try one of these combinations:

- **Apricot parrot tulips and coral ranunculus with guelder-rose**
- **Blue hyacinths and purple anemones with guelder-rose, berried ivy, catkins, and bergenia leaves**
- **Pink lilies, pale pink roses, and cherry blossom with guelder-rose and *Euphorbia***

If your garden is not bursting with suitable blooms, you can still achieve a natural effect by combining foliage, berries, and a few flowers from the garden with some gorgeous specimens from the florist (a case of literally having the best of both worlds). There's no need to try to pick up colors from your decor, as the unplanned nature of the bouquet is part of its charm. This type of loose, unstructured arrangement looks great in an entry hall, as it is friendly and informal.

In a contemporary interior, a simple glass vase of mixed blooms in just one color, or a massed arrangement of a single species, often looks better than a mixture of colors. It could either echo an accent color in the room or contrast with it. Again, it's a good idea not to add other, different-colored arrangements, or the impact could be diminished. In this setting, bold, graphic flowers like lilies, tulips, or amaryllis tend to work best. Surprisingly, white flowers can work well in a white decorating scheme, as the textures and shapes become more important. Whereas strong color could

possibly be a little jarring, the white arrangement is soft and serene. When a shot of color is needed, a little bright green or yellow-green from foliage or flowers can be combined with the white.

Use flowers in season whenever possible. These days, flower "arranging" involves not so much arranging the flowers as allowing them to fall into their own patterns, while just giving them the occasional tweak to adjust the shape. Tulips, of course, arrange themselves regardless, bending and twisting seemingly with a will of their own. When using flowers in a mixture of bright colors, position them in color groups rather than dotting them about, which dilutes their impact.

When arranging flowers for a table centerpiece, make sure that there will be room for the flowers once the

**ABOVE:** Bright flowers with plenty of foliage are casually bunched into two containers that contrast both in color and shape.

table is set and the food is there. Also, it's important that the display doesn't block sight lines when people are seated—a tall one is fine if the part of the arrangement at eye level is very narrow, otherwise the flowers should be short enough to see over. On a long table, two arrangements could be better, perhaps with a candelabra in the center. (If you replace one of the candles in the candelabra with a florist's candlecup—a very small plastic or metal cup that holds floral foam—you could incorporate tiny flowers or trailing stems.) Or you could have a long, low arrangement running down the center, which doesn't even need a container—just a pad of floral foam with waterproof backing. A variation on this would be a line of identical small containers, each containing flowers—or instead of a centerpiece, put a miniature vase with a few flowers at each person's place. Another idea is simply to lay ivy down the center of the tablecloth, and then sprinkle rosebuds and rose petals over the surface; you could also tie a sprig of ivy and a rosebud to each rolled-up napkin. Even quicker, arrange a line of small clay pots containing miniature topiary trees, flowering plants, or herbs down the center of the table.

## TOUCHING BASE

The container is often as important as the flowers:

- **Deep red gerberas in a black and gold lacquer vase**
- **White snowberries (*Symphoricarpos albus*) in a glass tank filled with small stones and seashells**
- **Pink and mauve sweet peas in a blue enamel cup**
- **Green foliage such as holly and cedar with red berries in a red glass vase**
- **White Amazon lilies or a Christmas rose in a silver-painted cast-iron container**

**RIGHT:** Boldly outlined against the light flooding in, a mass of branches bearing tiny green berries resembles a tree growing inside the large living room.

**ABOVE:** The color that flowers bring
into a room provides a delightful means
of echoing or accenting the decor.

# CANDLES

There is something reassuring in the fact that in our high-tech homes we still find candles the most attractive light source. It could be a deep-seated primeval attraction to fire, or the comforting sense of being within the intimate circle of illumination when seated at a candlelit dining table. Enveloped in the warm, soft glow and surrounded by flickering shadows, who could fail to enjoy the romantic ambience of candlelight?

The dining area is the prime spot for using candles. Glass or silver candlesticks or a candelabra can hold tapered, straight-sided, or twisted candles. They can even be fitted with little paper or fabric shades with metal frames that fit over the tops of the lit candles. Larger straight-sided candles, perhaps with colored patterns running through the wax, or candles molded into shapes such as pears or pine cones can be used in a floral centerpiece. Another option is to use floating candles (which come in shapes ranging from spheres to flat stars and fish) in a low bowl of water, accompanied by shells, sparkly beads, or floating flowers. Girandoles (wall sconces with mirror backing) and perhaps even a chandelier that holds candles could provide background candlelight.

In the living room, instead of a fire in the fireplace, chunky cream, brown, and gray candles of varying heights can be massed on the hearth, perhaps along with a fat, multi-wicked variety. (Use candle holders or place a tray underneath them to protect the hearth.) Beeswax candles can be used, too; made from thin amber-colored honeycomb sheets rolled into straight-sided or conical shapes, they are slow-burning and have a distinctive honey aroma. In an outdoor room, decorative pierced lanterns that hold candles can be hung overhead, as can colored glass votive holders. Scented votives in romantic little glass holders will add fragrance and atmosphere to the bathroom, while a huge scented candle in a floor-standing wood or iron church candlestick will do the same for the bedroom.

Never leave burning candles unattended: Impurities in the wax can sometimes result in too rapid burning and unexpected flare-ups.

**RIGHT:** As decorative features in their own right, candles ought to look good in the daytime, too. They are available with dried herbs and flowers applied to them, or you can simply tie on a sprig with ribbon, as here.

**RIGHT:** Whether classically simple or beautifully ornate, candlesticks look wonderful *en masse*.

## CANDLE POWER

Try some of these uses for candles:

- **To fill a room with fragrance, place scented votives among fragranced "pebble candles" (pebble-shaped paraffin-wax candles scented with essential oils) in a shallow dish.**
- **Stand beeswax candles in clay pots, holding them upright with sand or pebbles.**
- **Place a number of tapers (long, thin candles) in a bowl of sand, angling them to create a gently curved outline.**
- **Stand stubby candles in sand inside brown paper bags and use them to light the way up a drive or path at your next party.**

**BELOW:** Chunky candles bring real festive magic to this mantel decoration. The flames should always be kept well away from any flammable material.

# SEASONAL CHANGES

In the days before central heating and air conditioning, when homes were cold and drafty for much of the year, people were more responsive to the changing seasons. As the cold nights of fall arrived, preparations for the winter hibernation would begin, as homes were made as warm and cozy as possible. Then, in the spring, after all traces of winter had finally disappeared, the home was opened up once more to light and fresh air. By the time summer had arrived, people were ready, having adjusted their soft furnishings to keep the rooms as cool as possible and make the most of refreshing breezes.

Because our forebears were at the mercy of the elements more than we are, they had established a rhythm in their domestic lives that marked the changes occurring through the year. Their soft furnishings—wall and window hangings, slipcovers, and rugs and floorcloths—were never designed to remain the same, day in and day out: They were changed with the calendar. We can learn from our ancestors' example to make our homes more interesting. The motivation may now be a desire to be in harmony with nature, but that is just as valid.

With seasonal changes in the home you can simply do as much or as little as you like. However, you will find it easier if you have established a neutral canvas as your

**LEFT:** Fresh-looking cotton curtains, tablecloth, and chair skirts in a color scheme of pink, green, and white make this bright and cheerful dining room the epitome of springtime.

**BELOW:** Furniture as well as fabric can establish a seasonal keynote. This white-painted folding garden chair with its crisp pillow looks lighter and more summery than an "indoor" chair would.

## FABRIC FACELIFTS

Give your home a seasonal facelift by changing some of the pillows, throws, and other fabrics:

- **In winter, fake fur, fleece, chenille, and wool in rich patterns like paisley and strong plaids come into their own.**
- **Summer pillows and throws can be in lighter fabrics such as waffle weaves, piqué, and linen. There are many beautifully textured lightweight fabrics available.**

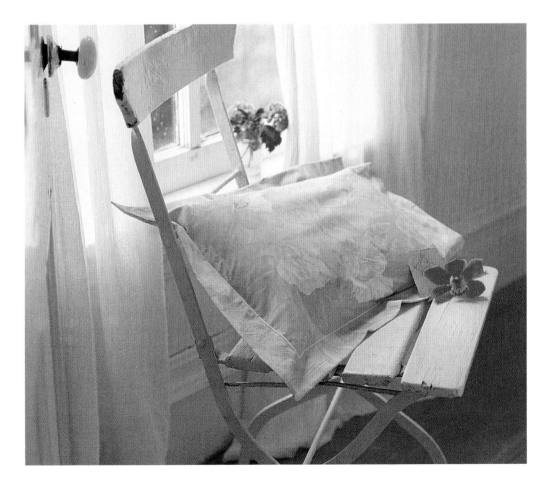

**RIGHT:** The yellow walls of this dining room can be part of a fall color scheme, as for this Thanksgiving dinner with its burnt-orange tablecloth and yellow accents, or else a light and bright decor for spring and summer.

**BELOW:** Furniture in a fresh blue and white color scheme is perfect for long, hot summer days. For winter, both of these chairs could be slipcovered, and the garden seat could either be replaced with a sofa or it, too, could be slipcovered, perhaps in a wool paisley or tweed, trimmed with a wool fringe. A plaid wool tablecloth and some seasonal branches and berries would complete the process of hunkering down for winter.

unchanging, year-round background, to which you can then make relatively superficial changes. Walls, floor coverings, and upholstery come into this category, as you won't want to change those twice a year, so follow the advice about neutral colors on pages 41–3. The seasonal changes discussed here are for summer and winter, but the same approach could be used to make changes in the spring and fall.

The first change to consider is whether to alter the focal point of your living room. In wintertime, most people like to focus on a fire, but during the hot days of summer, a leafy view of the garden is more appealing. Altering the furniture position to accommodate this, perhaps by just turning everything 90 degrees and making a few minor adjustments, will mean that the first transformation has cost nothing.

Fabric has always been the key to the majority of seasonal changes. In winter, heavy curtains that will shut out the sight of the cold, wet weather on those long, dark evenings help you feel warm and toasty, while in summer you want nothing more than sheers that will

## CHANGING TABLES

Table linen, too, can change with the seasons:

- **Choose light and airy muslin, linen, eyelet, or lace in white or pale, cool colors for tablecloths, place-mats, and napkins in the summer.**
- **In the winter, heavier weaves like tapestry, damask, or brocade in rich hues and patterns will look cozy and warm.**
- **Cushions or slip-covers for dining chairs can be changed to reflect the new look.**

## SEASONAL SLUMBER

Try these ideas to help your bedroom stay in tune with the seasons:

- **Use reversible coverlets with a richer color for winter and a pale side for summer.**
- **Drape muslin over the curtain pole and organdy over the dressing table to give the bedroom a cool luminosity in summer.**

waft in a gentle breeze. Taking down winter curtains and putting up sheers is not a major production, but an even easier approach is to have both layers in place permanently, and then simply keep tiebacks in place all the time in summer to hold the heavy curtains out of the way. This layered look is both practical and fashionable (see page 46). If you have installed a multi-track gliding panel system (see page 155), you could replace the panels according to the season, using, say, cool sheer linen or embroidered cotton in the summer and wool, velvet, chenille, suede, or damask in the winter.

Slipcovers are a terrific way of changing the look of your seating with the seasons. Any chair or sofa is a candidate, whether or not it is upholstered (see pages 72-3). You can have either two sets—one in rich, warm colors and snuggly textures for winter, the other in lighter, plainer cotton or linen for summer—or one set to change the look from the existing upholstery. Pillows and throws will probably need to be changed along with the slipcovers, since the fabrics used for them will relate to those used for the seating. However, this offers another good opportunity to bring in a new look for a new season (see box, page 247).

Despite the fact that they are not on show, bedrooms are the most important candidates for a seasonal makeover. Not only does the atmosphere affect your psychological state, but the bed is where physical comfort will be affected by the accessories. Obviously you'll need to replace warm blankets, quilts, comforters, or duvets with lightweight covers, but if the bed has hangings, these could be changed, too. In summer, heavy bed curtains will be even more unwelcome than on the windows, so they could be removed so that the frame stands bare and bold, or replaced with organdy, muslin, voile or other floaty, gauzy curtains.

Finally, don't forget the impact seasonal flowers can have in bringing the outdoors inside (see page 240). By making some of these changes, you will be not only adapting your home to the world outside, but also refreshing the decor. Seasonal makeovers help to insure that your living space is always evolving.

**CHRISTMAS CHIC**
Like flowers, potted plants and accessories also reflect the time of year. At Christmas, elegant miniature topiary trees and wreaths bound with gold ribbon can be used like any other item of furnishing to lend a yuletide flavor to the home without sacrificing style.

# INDEX

Page numbers in *italics* indicate captions.

# ACKNOWLEDGEMENTS

The author would particularly like to thank Janet James for her inspiring and hard-working design, and both Janet and Corinne Asghar for their non-stop patience and cheerfulness.